FAITH IN OUR FREEDOM

10 Refugee Families, 1 Determined woman & Faith beyond imagination

True Stories that will inspire and fill your heart with love and compassion

AUTHOR:
ANGELIQUE PAPADELIAS

Acknowledgements

I would firstly like to thank the amazing group of individuals who helped make this project a reality. Without a dedicated and highly competent team from Canada, Mexico, Venezuela, Argentina, Greece and Australia, we could not have achieved such an exceptional result.

Jocelyn **Legaré***: Through Jocelyn I met the children of several refugee families in the area and was introduced to Line Chaloux.*

Valérie LeBlanc*: Valérie arranged all the initial meetings with the refugee families and co-ordinated the required interview translators so that I could ask my questions and fully understand the refugee stories.*

Janot Bélanger*: Janot was my principal French to English interview translator who dedicated many hours of his time to help with this project. Janot attended many of the longer interviews with Line and the families.*

Roxanne **Beaupré***: Roxanne assisted with two French to English family interview translations.*

Nathalie*: Nathalie assisted with one Spanish to English family interview translation.*

Nirmala Bastola*: Nirmala assisted with one Nepali to English family interview translation.*

Véronique Cyr*: Véronique assisted with one French to English family interview translation.*

Stephanie McLean *(Australia): Stephanie conducted the entire edit of the English version, bringing her expertise in editing and her exceptional grammatical and research skills to the stories in order to clarify the exact element discussed within each story.*

Linda Cadieux: *Linda's continuous moral support encouraged me to keep moving forward to bring this project to fruition.*

Annie Leroux: *Annie highlighted Line's achievements and persisted on the need to tell Line's story in order to recognize her exceptional work within the community in the Laurentians Region.*

Lyon Leshley: *Lyon offered feedback and support to the final version and formatted the ebook for publishing and marketing purposes.*

The 'Spanish Version' Translators

Mirta Rodriguez: *(Montreal) Mirta contributed to translating Chapter Eleven of Line's story in the French Version as well as all of Part Three (Line's Story) in the Spanish Version. A very dedicated woman.*

Adriana Herrera *(Argentina): Adriana contributed to translating one third of the book.*

Rocio Tamez: *(Mexico / Montreal) Rocio contributed to translating the first section, Chapter Sixteen, Chapter Fifteen and the entire Part I of the book. An extraordinary effort by her.*

Natalia Linares: *(Venezuela) Natalia contributed to translating one of the refugee stories within the book.*

Maria Fikari: *(Greece) Maria contributed to translating the blurb of the book cover.*

The Spanish Version Editor

Rocio Tamez was responsible for the edit / proof read of the Spanish Translation.

The French Version Translators

Prudence Assogba: *(Montreal) Prudence contributed to translating, Chapter Three, Twelve until Fifteen and Part Two of the entire book. An extremely efficient and supportive effort.*

Makraphone Phouttama: *(Montreal): Makra contributed to translating the first section of the book until the end of Chapter One, and Chapter Five.*

Francois Luc Paradis: *(Montreal) Francois contributed to translating Chapter Four of the book.*

Myrlene Metellus: *(Montreal) Myrlene contributed to translating Chapter Two of the book.*

Anastasia Oikonomopoulou: *(Greece) Anastasia contributed to translating the blurb of the book.*

Bichara Coussa: *(Montreal) Richard translated a section that was added to the original prologue.*

The French Version Editors

David Mendes Da Silva: *(Montreal) David was responsible for the first raw edit of Part One of the book, making sure all the translations were uniform. He also translated Chapter Sixteen, the campaign material and is a very supportive individual.*

Prudence Assogba: *(Montreal) Prudence conducted one of the final proof reads of the book.*

Denis Cyr: *Denis assisted with some final grammatical checks.*

Lyne Rochon: *Lyne conducted the final proof read of the French version.*

To each of you above, I strongly wish you all the best success in life. Thank you for your kind hearts, generous time and commitment to completing this project. Without your skills, knowledge and amazing efforts to complete this book, it would not have been completed in the time frame required. I am proud to have worked with all of you and had you all part of the team. Well done.

Fund Raising Campaign Promotional Team:

Thank you to Paul Leiba, Annie Guillemette, Sihem Oka, Veronique Cyr, Veronique Beaulieu, Santa Maya Sharma, Line Chaloux and Mr Jonas that helped film some footage to help promote the videos for the crowd funding campaign.

Contributors: To each individual that contributed to the crowd funding campaign, either through sharing our work with your friends and/or donating financially, it was through your generous assistance that we got here and I wish to thank you for supporting us at that time.

Those contributors are:

Gianpietro Tiberio, Helen Syrmalis, Christina Galanopoulos, Paul Leiba, Denis Cyr, Julian Galea, Virginia Villar, Eva Psaltis, Angie Karipidis, Patty Apostolidis, Louis Cadieux, Greek Refugee Forum, Katie Lowden, Maria Papas, Monique Cyr - Laframboise, Ghislaine Cyr, Linda Cadieux, Joseph Malouf, Joanna Mangos, Anthony and Emma Colfelt, Rachel Bower, Cristina Carvana, Kelly whalen, Jeff Collins, Stephanie Lagradelle, Rhonda Yim, Effie Mahanidis, Nicole Borzelleca, Mari-Luis Agius, Melanie Coombs, Lesley Kelman Koeppel, Irene Papadelias, Renee Sotile, Nia Angeles, Maria Longo, Amanda Hale, Tess Cassar, Leah Stylianou – Karlis, Natasha Sotirios, Angie Karipidis, Vicki Fassoulis Bruneau, Sophie Lajoie and Gina Tapinos Atcheson

CONTENTS

Acknowledgements

Prologue

Part I

Part II

Part III

PROLOGUE

There are people that I have met, often unexpectedly, who do so much for others that I often sit quietly and reflect on them in awe and amazement. If just one person can achieve so much in a lifetime, imagine what changes we could make if we all found our purpose in life at an early age and worked diligently to realize that goal. The likely reality is that we are all here on our own journeys. How connected we are to ourselves, our spirituality or inner self and our fellow beings; will determine how we live our life journey and at what pace we will move until we each find our purpose in life.

I choose to live my life by being a voice of the people and that is why I continue to write, create films and interact with people in order to share the life experiences of others. I do not have a fear of traveling and relocating, meeting new people and developing new friendships, undergoing new experiences or spending time by myself. This leads me to explore new cultures and novel philosophies, to hear others' views on life and to place myself in a position where I question everything that I have grown up believing and I can embrace what it is that I truly accept within my own soul. It is healthy to live with an open mind and I try to achieve this so that I can identify and accept what the universe is offering me.

I know that for some people life is tough, every day is a battle. The intensity of the battles depends on their life until the present and how prepared they are to fight for the future that they want for themselves. Others have been bought into a life that is filled with love, compassion and understanding, rarely experiencing too many moments of major adversity. No matter where we come from and no matter into which side of the spectrum we fall, what is important is how we are with others, how we sit with ourselves and how we can learn to open our hearts to people all over the world and spread the message of love. With love we can fight war. With love in our hearts, we can challenge even the toughest of enemies. We are all capable of feeling that love, being that love and seeing the light that will fill our hearts with that love.

When I came to Canada, I wondered what the universe was thinking, sending mc to a country where the snow is so bitterly cold and the winters seem to be so long. Even though my entire family are of Greek origin, they migrated to Australia and I was born and raised in the coastal areas of New South Wales. I never played with snow or built snow men. I was at the beach, building sandcastles, playing sport and paddling out into the ocean, feeling the salt water over my skin, working in the family business and sun bathing for much of the year. It was a good, comfortable life, my family worked hard and I felt extremely blessed to be born and raised in Australia.

Education and awareness are key to initiate change. I began by studying a Bachelor of Education and went on to teach children and adults for over ten years. I have been fortunate enough to teach in Australia, the island of Fiji and recently volunteered to help teach refugee children in Quebec, Canada.

My experience teaching in Fiji taught me how to adapt my lessons in poorer environments and to be flexible with limited resources. All children are beautiful. Their innocence and curiosity continuously astounds me. When we educate children, we are investing in a better future for communities everywhere.

In my mid 20s' I trained and served in the New South Wales Police Force in Australia for eight years and I was exposed to suffering on a daily basis. Throughout my policing experience I dealt with many cases that opened my eyes to the atrocities that occur in society. The impact on victims suffering from mental illness, domestic violence and assaults, allowed me realize the significance of all protection laws and their effectiveness when implemented.

I progressed to train in Criminal Analysis and Strategic Intelligence (CASIC). I was exposed to larger scale criminal operations such as human trafficking, drug trafficking, mass murders and riot situations. I even attended a refugee detention centre and was educated about the issues that many refugees and migrants face when they initially arrive in other communities and face local authorities such as police for the first time. The 'policing' world had a significant impact into the way I now view the world in which we all live and the complexities to consider when planning to implement change that affects people's lives.

Once in my 30's, I felt a strong change inside me but it took a few years for those feelings and thoughts to develop into action. By 2011, I had changed careers to explore my creative side and after completing a Film Producing and Directing course, I was selected into the emerging Producers scheme with the Screen Producers Association of Australia (SPAA) and from there I was awarded a position into a scholarship program in Sydney to study Multi platform and Transmedia producing. Once I had completed my studies, I set up a business called Little Screen Big Screen to platform my creative work. This change guided my next decision. I could choose to exist in the same space, in my own comfort zone and have a happy, ordinary life or I could choose to shake it up a little, leave the familiarity behind and go out into the world and embrace what is out there.

I wasn't initially bound for Canada; I left Australia to discover New York. This was such a different world from where I was raised and, in time, I learnt to love what the city offered and the dynamic and magnetic energy force that surrounds it. Spurred on by a city full of transitioning people, I could feel the desire to move forward. For me, New York was a place that set me up for the road ahead. It was there that I realized that my purpose in life was to be the voice of people. In October 2012, when Hurricane Sandy hit the state of New York, I went out into the hurricane, facing my first natural disaster to see what I could do to help. By facing the storm head on, I was facing my fears and by facing my fears, my purpose in life started to become very clear.

Helping several charity organizations, I delivered food and resources to people in need in a city and country that I barely knew. I remember loving every moment of being involved. After opening their doors to me, they then also opened themselves to me. They began to tell me their stories and I genuinely began to listen to them, hearing about their painful experiences, their loss, their needs and their fears. I created a documentary on their stories titled, 'Foreign Eye in the Storm'. It was well received in the film festivals in New York and New Jersey and it was my way of nurturing and helping to heal the people in that community who wanted to talk to a stranger about their terrible ordeals. I went there to help them but it was they who helped me. It is now available on Amazon and Vimeo on

9

Demand for rental or purchase.

During this time, I connected with a man who approached me to write his life story. I spent a considerable amount of time with him, capturing every element of his personality and recording his life's journey. He had a strong desire to share his story with the world and, without hesitation, thinking it was a sign to move forward, I began my next venture. That year was a bumpy road along which I learnt patience, endurance and how to remain focused at all times. It was a challenging and interesting period of time but I knew that all the experiences and lessons learnt along that path were setting me up for a far greater journey ahead.

In New York, I met the love of my life who inspired me to move to Canada and begin to have our own family. I immediately felt a strong connection to Saint Sauveur, a quaint town to the North of Montreal. After spending some time in the region I discovered Piedmont and that is where we were married. I knew that there was something drawing me to this place. I had very few friends locally, I couldn't speak a single word of French and I was far away from everyone who had played such a large part in my life. My family, life-long friends and little dog Charlie were all on the other side of the world but I knew I had to be here.

When we settled into our new life, I met some interesting people, one of whom was a woman who told me that she worked as a teacher and helped many young refugee children settle into school in Canada. I had an overwhelming feeling tugging at my soul to meet these children. I did not know why, I just knew I needed to meet them.

I went to the school, met the children with their smiling little eyes filled with hope. Many of them could not understand a word that I said but, in reality, no words were needed. When I looked into the faces of one particular little Columbian boy and one little African girl, their eyes told me stories that I knew I needed to explore.

Soon afterwards, I met with the lady that had established the immigration and refugee center in the local area. She was absolutely extraordinary. We developed an instant rapport and I felt that I found a long lost sister. Her name is Line Chaloux and meeting her is one of life's great gifts to me. I had previously spoken to several people in the community who praised her unreservedly and all could not understand how she managed to accomplish everything that she set out to do. I was intrigued to discover more and to know how one woman could instigate so much change in one area.

Every moment I spent with Line was like a moment in my childhood when I met an inspiring teacher or watched an amazing actress deliver an extraordinary performance. I was utterly moved, waiting to hear her every word and experience so that I could understand how she developed into the person that she is today. Even though she speaks limited English, through the wonderful translation provided by Janot, I could fully understand Line's every word and relate to her love of mankind which was expressed so fully during our conversations. It was not at all difficult to realize the reasons for Line's success and why she is such a special person. The Native American bloodline of the Clan of the Turtle runs through her body and inspires her soul. Is it this spiritual connection that makes this incredible woman so patient and so dedicated to the cause of helping refugees escape the horrors to which they are exposed in order to have the chance of freedom in another country? In my eyes, Line belongs to a small and exclusive family of human angels around the world who choose to devote their lives to helping others.

At the same time I was approached to write another biography, which meant I needed to travel to Mexico. I had the most amazing spiritual transformation in Mexico and by the time I came back, everything had crystallized in my mind as to my exact purpose in life. I had to ensure that when I wrote, they were stories that conveyed important messages. Messages of love, peace and compassion for ourselves and others. Messages that inspired people and bought them to find the light and love in their hearts. I decided that I would no longer spend my time writing for people whose agendas were not totally pure of heart.

Within those first few weeks after returning from Mexico, and with the help of Valérie, an extremely dedicated liaison, I met the families of the refugee children and began to write the story of their lives. I was motivated, inspired and I felt I needed to meet more families. I spent time with ten refugee families and listened to their stories. The families are from Kosovo, Colombia, Bhutan and Africa. I felt that I would be able to relate to their anxieties and concerns of moving to a foreign country but nothing prepared me for what they had gone through beforehand.

Many of us are caught up in the dramas of our own lives and the issues that we consider at the time to be a major challenge. We overlook how lucky we are to have grown up in first world countries where we have comfortable accommodation, an abundance of food, many personal possessions, a good education, government benefits and opportunities for healthcare. Having had just such a background, I never understood the global refugee crisis and had no idea of the extreme hardships that millions of refugees all over the world face on a daily basis.

The biggest gift I can give these people is to share their stories with a global audience. Their stories are filled with pain and suffering but will show that with determination and strong faith, anything is possible.

It is an honor to write this entire story and I thank Line and the refugee families for allowing me to tell their stories. I sincerely hope that through these stories, I can encourage others around the world to open their hearts to refugees and welcome them into their countries, local areas and communities and help them to integrate so that they understand our way of living and that we can appreciate the differences in each others lives. Let us open our hearts with love and compassion to these families and their beautiful children and always remember why they are here.

An important comment: Some of the refugee names from Africa and Columbia have been changed for the purposes of safety and security. I have tried to maintain the same level of language expressed to me by these families throughout each story. I have stayed faithful to the version of events as provided to me by each of the families. In some of the stories, the personal accounts of some events (and their cause) differ from recorded references found in other publications or media. However, these are their stories and their personal memories. Many refugees flee their homes at a very young age and it is their recollections of events that stay with them throughout their entire life.

PART I

REFUGEE STORIES I

Chapter I

Nepali Refugee from Bhutan

My Name is Lachu Man and I was born in 1982 in the village of Gopini in the district of Tsirang (formerly Chirang), Bhutan. I was the baby of the family, the youngest of four boys, each born two years apart. We lived with our parents in our rural home in the southern part of the country which enjoys a milder climate than many other parts of the country. My brothers and I helped with growing food produce on our land.

By 1990 the situation for the Lhotsampas, as we the people of Nepalese descent are known, deteriorated dramatically. I was only 8 years old at the time so my memories are limited. The king ordered that no person speak Nepalese and that Nepali be removed from schools as a language of instruction. He further ordered that all were to wear local Bhutanese outfits in any public place. Many older Nepalese people that my family knew decided to protect our culture and religion by approaching the authorities to request that we be allowed to keep our cultural and traditional practices. Some people formed groups and went to complain to government officials directly. Many participated in anti-government rallies.

The orders remained in place and the Dupas army, starting from the western side of Bhutan, crossed the country and entered villages looking for any protestors. Those that were identified were killed or physically beaten and imprisoned. Girls between the ages of ten to nineteen were systematically raped and told to leave. The army was a strong force, sent to drive us all out of the country. We were stripped of our cultural liberties and the right to call Bhutan our home. It had become extremely unsafe to live in our homeland.

As we were living in the southern part of Bhutan, news reached us about what was happening to our people in the west. My father took the decision to protect his family from this persecution and to escape from Bhutan.

We left our home with a little money that my father had saved and we walked for two days with no food or water until we arrived at the Indian border. There were other families that also left on the same day and no-one knew what would happen to us. Once we crossed the border my father paid a truck driver to transport us to one of the temporary refugee camps called Morang in Nepal. After arriving there, we were later assigned to the Sanischare camp which was one of the seven permanent camps. The others were Beldangi 1, Beldangi 2, Beldangi 3, Goldhap, Khudunabari and Timai. There were approximately 100,000 Nepalese refugees from Bhutan in these camps.

LOCATION MAP OF CAMPS

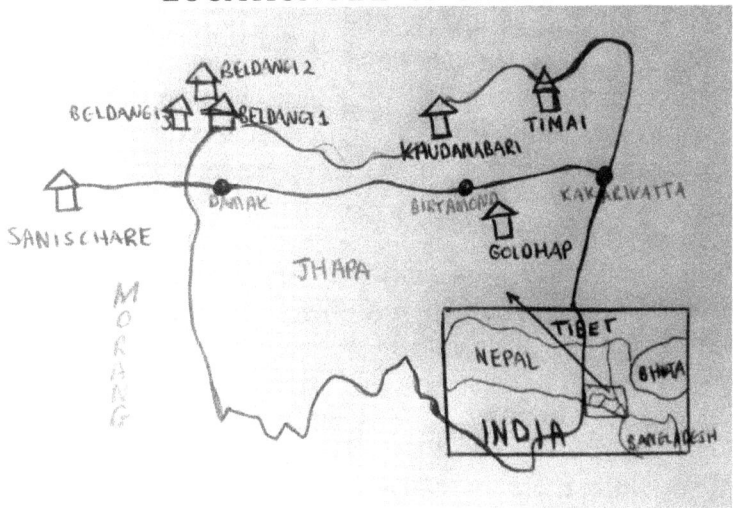

When we arrived we were given bamboo, one sheet of plastic and some tools to construct a hut. My older brothers helped my father build this very basic home for us. I often saw my parents crying. They were absolutely devastated about losing everything they had worked for their whole lives. We had left everything behind and now we had nothing. We had no clothes and none of the basic necessities. My brothers and I cried along with our parents.

A great number of people died in these camps purely from the scarcity of food and from the dramatic change in environment. The weather was very hot in Nepal and we were not used to these warmer temperatures.

We had no choice but to accept the change. A car with a loudspeaker drove around the camp updating us on any news. There were no official rules about behavior in the camp; everybody was living in a place of sorrow so it was peaceful and calm. No one quarreled, no one stole from another and, as time went by, people started doing small jobs and some people even made things to sell inside the camp. No one could leave the camp to work and no one from outside the camp could come in.

Although we were not allowed to leave the camp for work, by 1992 we were allowed to walk to the local river to take a bath and wash our clothes. It took half an hour to walk to the river. My older brother eventually managed to get himself a bicycle and I would borrow it to ride to the river. We went to the river at different times of the day depending on whether there was water available inside the camp.

The water in the camp was distributed in many different sectors from Sector A to Sector L. In sector A, there were four sections, A1, A2, A3 and A4. In each section there were two taps where the water was distributed. The water was available three times a day for only one hour at a time. Two people from every family would go and stand in line with a bucket. The wait time was from half an hour to one hour in the morning, afternoon and evening. At times it was difficult to get the water because there were long lines of people waiting and time ran out. My mother used the water to cook and prepare meals. If there was water remaining, we could wash ourselves under the hut. Every so often they would clean the area around the water taps and during this time, we would either get water from another sector – rarely was there enough for everyone – or we had no choice but to go to the river. We were like fish living out of water, but still breathing. It was the most difficult time of our lives.

There was a school and a small hospital inside the camp. Once I started school at the camp, I was a lot happier for having the diversion of learning something new. I started to make friends at school and that was also a nice change. The hospital in the camp was very basic and there was a constant lack of doctors to cope with the large number of people.

At times when the rain and winds came, the water would drip inside the hut and soak our beds. We couldn't sleep as everything was saturated. When the wind blew the plastic off our roof we couldn't go to school the next day due to not having had sufficient sleep. Times were tough on everybody and once the rain stopped, we had to dry our beds. They would give us more bamboo, another plastic sheet and my brothers would help my father construct another shelter. This process took 2-3 days.

There was always a scarcity of food and water. The UN would transport food trucks to the camp and distribute staples such as rice, oil, onions, pumpkin, chilli, lentils and bananas. It was up to us to buy meat and other vegetables with the little money we could get from small jobs. We could not leave the camp to get other food so whatever we were given, we accepted. When the water ran out, we would have no water to cook rice so we could not eat sufficiently and had poor nutrition, which led to a lack of concentration at school and hunger pains. Years later, the UN started to provide us with breakfast at the school which was cooked in a small kitchen and could be best described as 'wheat powder' porridge. Life at the time was like that of a camel living in the dessert without food but carrying water on its back to survive.... and at many times, without the water.

My father needed to earn some money for us so he became a 'pastor' in the camp. We were of the Hindu faith. He would walk to peoples' homes, reading and praying with them and they would give him a small amount of money for his services. That money was used for our food.

The government of Nepal continued to have meetings with the King of Bhutan to negotiate our return but he would not agree.

By the year 2000 we were allowed to leave the camps but still not permitted to do any work. My uncle went outside to attempt to work in the local area but was caught by the police who imprisoned him for six months.

My brothers all found wives, built their own huts and started having their own families. I kept going to school and I remember my teacher telling us that one day we will return to our country and begin our lives again. He would fill us with hope and courage about creating a better life for ourselves, that survival through tough times and difficulties could lead to success and that if we continued with our education, one day we would be rich and in a good place. He repeated this to us regularly. We had many different teachers but this particular one was inspiring. The teachers at the camp lived inside the camp so they understood and related to everything that we were going through.

The teachers also organized school programs and festivals inside the camp and we were able to watch these dramatic acts and sing along with the performers. My friend Krishna, who loved to sing and write lyrics and poems, would participate in them. I valued his friendship. We children learnt so much from these school spectaculars and also from the older children at the school.

In that same year of 2000, an announcement was made at our camp that students in Class 11 and 12 could do six months of computer training in the local town. I had just finished class 10 so I qualified and walked with my friends to the local school in town. We would go five days a week for 1-2 hours at a time. When we first saw the computers we were overjoyed. It was such a nice feeling to see other Nepalese people outside of the camp but often they would harass and dominate us "Ah, Bhutanese, get out of here". People from the camp were often beaten up by local Nepalese if out walking alone at night.

Upon finishing Class 12, students were permitted to tutor smaller children at the camp. I did this and got paid around 2000 rupees a month, approximately $24-$26 Canadian dollars per month. This was the only job I had at the camp during my time there.

When I had a little spare money saved from working, my friends and I would go to the local cinema outside the camp. Announcements were made over the loudspeaker at the camp as to what film was playing. It cost 20 rupees and as that was a lot of money for us, we only went to see a film twice a year. It took one hour to walk there but I loved the experience. My best friends were Madan Giri and Krishna and we would read in class together and go to the cinema when we could. One day we watched a Nepalese film that was called something similar to "Dignity". We learnt so much watching those films: we saw how people respected one another, how people co-operated in the outside world and how we could work and develop our lives. We would see how love was shown between parents and children and at times we watched documentaries based on human nature, love and relationships.

Many of the movies were Bollywood films with singing, dancing and romance but some were action movies. The cinema accommodated around 500 people inside the building and there was a mixture of plastic and wooden chairs on which to sit. Walking back home, we would discuss and critique the film in minute detail. The film would stay in our memories for a very long time afterwards as it would be a long time between our cinema outings.

At school, I was close to a girl who I was convinced would be my future wife; so she too became a special friend. We would also occasionally watch a film at the cinema. I remember we watched "Darpan Chaya" which in English is titled "The Illusory Mirror" and is still considered one of Nepal's best and largest-grossing movies. That was my favorite film because it talked about family, love and education.

I fell in love with her. By the time I was 21 years of age, I had sent her several love letters but she rejected the first and second and wouldn't agree to be with me. By the third letter, she agreed to spend more time with me to determine exactly what type of person I was. Her love towards me grew and, in time, she said yes to my letters and agreed to be with me. My father and I walked to her hut to ask her father for his daughter's hand in marriage. We then had to wait a few days for a response. In Nepalese culture, dowries are common practice. When a man asks for someone's daughter in marriage, he is allowed to make a request for something material, even something like a motorcycle. In the camp, no one had anything to give so requests were not made. The family accepted our proposal and we were married on the 1st January 2005.

It was such an exciting time because my father gave us the little money he had saved from his prayer readings and we went to the market to buy my future wife a red sari, the color worn by brides at weddings. It was beautiful and dotted with beads. I wore a black coat and pants. Musicians played at our modest but lovely wedding. My wife came to live with my parents and me in our humble hut and took our family name.

Family and friends at our wedding

By the end of that year, our first son was born and even though we were very happy, parenting in the camp was very challenging because of the scarcity of food. The UN gave us some baby food to help us but it was difficult to obtain the rest of the things that are needed for a baby.

In 2007, I was bitten by a mosquito and contracted malaria. I became very sick, experiencing a terrible fever and pain in my muscles and aches in my bones. At first my wife looked after me but when the shaking and fever increased, she took me to the hospital for treatment. I was given an injection which worked relatively quickly and made me feel much better.

My mother contracted tuberculosis. I remember seeing her in a bad state, bleeding from the mouth and sweating from the fever. Often we needed to get her to the hospital in a hurry but we weren't strong enough to carry her. My friends Madan Giri and Krishna would help me put her on a bicycle to wheel her to the hospital. At times, if no-one else was available, my wife would help me transport my mother. We all had to wear masks around her for six months during her treatment. Fortunately, we didn't have to pay for medicine which was a god-send. This was a tough period in our lives.

My wife and I had discussed returning to Bhutan but we knew we couldn't. None of us wanted to stay in the camp anymore. We wanted a better and brighter life. In 2007, the officials agreed to allow us to go to other countries. We sat down as a family to decide which country we would go. As we wanted to find a peaceful country and preferably a cooler climate, which would remind us of our home in Bhutan, we chose to go to Canada and lodged our applications with the International Organization for Migration (OIM).

By 2008, refugees were allowed to leave the camp to work but even though I had finished all my studies to Class 12 level, it was impossible for me to obtain a government office job. The government of Nepal did not want to give their good jobs to Nepalese refugees. This convinced us that we should leave.

Although my wife's family decided on the USA and were successful in their application, we kept to the plan of going to Canada. It was a lonely time for my wife when her family left but we had our own happy little family. Our visa for Canada was sent to the camp and soon afterwards my parents, one of my brothers and my immediate family were on a bus to the airport, followed by several flights to Montreal.

We were both happy and sad to leave Nepal. We were leaving our family, friends, neighbors and relatives but we knew that this was the opportunity to make a better life for our family. In Canada, we have freedom, equality and everything we need. This wonderful country offers endless possibilities.

One year after we arrived, my other brothers joined us in Canada. We all assemble together to celebrate birthdays and other special occasions. We are all very happy.

It took us some time to learn French but we managed. I was told to go to an adult school to undertake Secondary One and now with government help in vocational training, I was able to study to become an assistant chef. I want to run my own business one day so I am working hard towards that goal. We had our second son here in Canada and it is a very different experience giving birth to and raising a child in this country.

We plan on saving some money so that one day we can go to the USA and visit my wife's family. We will need to pass our citizen test before that can happen. I often recall the hard times that we experienced in Bhutan and Nepal and will always be grateful for the beautiful life that we can now enjoy in freedom.

I was in the camp since I was eight years old. I am now 32 years old and my wife is 31. I spent twenty long years in that camp and now, with our new-found freedom, we look forward to the road ahead.

Chapter II

Refugee from the Democratic Republic of the Congo (DRC)

My name is Abebe and I was born in the village of Kabare, situated in the province of North–Kivu (Nord-Kivu) in the eastern part of the Democratic Republic of the Congo, also known as the DRC. I was born in the local public hospital which had limited resources but still functioned effectively as a birthing facility. My father had two wives. One wife gave birth to two children. The second wife, my birth mother had seven children, all born in the DRC. Two of her daughters died at a young age due to disease. One of my brothers died a few years ago from an infection in his leg. Only four boys remain now and apart from me, the rest of them still live in the DRC. I look different to my siblings. My skin is a lot darker, my face and nose are much thinner compared to my brothers who have larger and wider noses like the Bantu people of our Bashi Tribe.

I was born in late 1964, just after the War of Independence from Belgium. There were so many political issues at the time and it is quite confusing and difficult to try and understand them all. It was around the time that I was born that President Mobutu came into power in 1965 as leader of the country. The area where we were located became reasonably peaceful at that time.

By the time I was three years old, my father became terribly sick and he passed away in 1967. I do not remember this period of time but as I grew older, I remember having a deep love and respect for my mother as she took on both parenting roles.

My eldest brother helped my mother at times by attending to such issues as the paperwork for me to be enrolled in school. I loved school. I loved learning and it was a great joy to go to school.

When I was six years old I contacted measles. My body was covered in spots and the disease affected my right eye. My eyeball started to grow rapidly and when they took me to the local hospital, it was not equipped with enough medical staff and resources to treat me. My mother then took me to the hospital in the town of Bukavu.

A group of Belgian doctors were based there and they were qualified eye specialists. They informed us that because my eyeball had grown beyond the eye socket, it would have to be removed. I accepted this as an incident of circumstance and agreed for them to operate on my eye. I remember having the mask placed over my face and losing consciousness. Being so young at the time, it was an exceptional experience.

When I awoke, they were carrying me on a stretcher to my room. I recovered well and for the following two weeks the doctors visited me everyday to check on my progress. I felt a lot better once my eye had healed and the pain had gone.

I was still considered the best student in my class after that. Even with my one eye. I continued to be first in my class.

I had a great relationship with my mother. She looked after all of us and always had food prepared for us when it was meal time. My eldest brother met a woman whom he married. She came to live with us but it wasn't easy. My father had left us his piece of land and we had three small houses on the land. My brother lived with his wife and my mother in one house. My other brothers and I shared the other two houses and at times we would sleep in the same bed.

My brother's wife was not happy in this household and there were always problems with her. It was hard on my brother because he would take his wife's side and that created problems for my mother.

The rest of us got along very well. When my older brother was away with his wife, I remember laughing at the stories my mother would tell us about how she grew up and her point of view about things in general. We were a family with a strong Christian faith and my mother would always teach us how to behave in society and the importance of having a good education. I share her beliefs that if you educate your family, you are educating your country because you are educating its citizens, and therefore you are educating the world. If there are many criminals in this world, it is because they have failed to be educated within their family unit. We need to make sure we are managing the day to day situations within our own families.

I didn't have any relationships with women when I was a teenager. I never found anyone with whom I fell in love. I never drank or partied as I believed that if I drank alcohol and slept with women I would catch a disease and I didn't want that.

My brothers and I had many dinners as a family and one night, my mother told me a story to help me find a wife. She explained to me that it was important to meet a woman who was tall, like my mother. In her opinion, if I found a woman who was short, I would be unhappy because she wouldn't be able to help me with everything. She gave me an example of a man wanting to smoke tobacco and needing a light. If your wife is too short, she wouldn't be able to help me light it so it was important for us both to be the same height so that we could help each other. Her viewpoint was that if the woman couldn't help, she would develop a complex. She believed that short people have complexes that cause them to be mean to people. I grew up with her stories and remember what a joy it was to listen to her theories and to have had that sacred time with her.

She refused to marry again because she wanted to spend her time taking care of us and being there for us. Her love for us was beautiful.

Over the years, I continued to study and then, in 1982 when I was eighteen years old, I decided to leave for the city of Bukavu in South-Kivu province. I wanted to further my studies at university with the aim of obtaining a business management degree. I was also interested in teaching so I also undertook studies in teaching. I settled in a home and went to church every Sunday.

When I completed my studies after several years, it was hard to find related work in the DRC. At times, I needed to take jobs in other regions so that I had an income to support myself. I did this for many years.

When I was 33 years old I remember going to church and seeing a girl and I fell in love. I had a good relationship with the pastors and went to speak to them about her. In our religion, if we were attracted to a girl, we were not meant to approach her and declare our love. We had to go through the pastor. The reasoning behind this was that if there was another brother in Christ who had seen her first and another man made a move for her, it could create enemies and lead to confrontation. The pastors wanted to avoid this situation so people were asked to go through the pastors to speak with their prospective wives.

When I spoke with the pastor for the first time I said, "You see that woman, I want to talk to her, I love her". I went home and I was so impatient waiting for their response. I spoke to my mother about her and it took three weeks for the pastor to come back and tell me that I could speak with her. It was so nice to finally meet up with her.

I prepared a love letter stating my love for her and told her that if she didn't love me back, she didn't need to accept my offer of marriage. However, she said yes and six months later, in May 1996, we were married. She was beautiful and my mother was happy because she was tall.

We had a big celebration at the church in Bukavu with prayers and a service that started at 9 a.m. and lasted three hours. After the church service, we travelled 25kms back to my birth village for a big feast. We received many gifts from my brothers and it was a joyous time. We stayed there for two months so that my wife and I could spend time with my family and develop a good relationship with all.

By the time we left the village to go back to the city of Bukavu, my wife was pregnant. It was during this time that the first of many wars began and we were living in extreme fear. The war reached our city and we needed to find a safer place to live so we decided to return to my birth village. We loaded a few belongings on our heads and we ran. We had to run the entire 25 kilometers and there were men, women and children running in every direction. People had been shot and their corpses were piled up around us. We were climbing over people's bodies to run as far away as possible. My wife was suffering terribly and it wasn't long before she lost the baby through miscarriage. When we arrived at our village, we settled in for two months in order to give my wife time to heal. We prayed that the hand of God was with her and that she would recover.

Many people from the city came back to the village but it didn't take long for the war to reach our village. To escape from the hostilities, we returned to Bukavu and my wife again fell pregnant. We settled in our home and I began working in the area. After nine months, I was at work and received a message that my wife was giving birth at the hospital. I went immediately to be with her. It was such an amazing experience to see our first born child. I felt so special, that I was good enough to have been blessed with a child. When I saw my little baby girl, I kissed her warmly. My wife and I hugged each other and thanked the lord for this wonderful blessing. We were very, very happy.

We left the hospital the next day and it was time to celebrate the new life in our family. When there is birth, we always celebrate the newborn and we invite our family, friends and neighbors to join us in the celebrations. All the family came to visit us at our home and relatives bought gifts such as money, rice, sugar, soaps and clothing for the baby. We ate and danced all day.

It wasn't long after our child was born, that my wife fell pregnant again. I needed to make more money to support my growing family. I had small jobs but the government system was bad at paying their employees so I had to take jobs further away. It was tough because it meant that my wife was alone to take care of first child and she was pregnant with our second.

I was offered a job 500 kilometers away in the town of Moba, with a Not for Profit Organization doing their accounting. I caught a plane to get there because there were no proper roads to get there. When I needed to go anywhere, I had no other choice but to fly.

I enjoyed working in Moba and I made some friends at work and through the church. I spoke with my wife as often as I could until communication was limited because the war had reached my town. I managed to receive a message that my wife had just given birth to our second daughter and I was so happy to hear the news. I wanted to go back to my wife and daughters but with the streets full of soldiers and civil unrest, it was unsafe to try and flee.

However, I decided to go and I was stopped and arrested by soldiers accusing me that I was from Rwanda. I told them I was from the Congo and I just looked different. They didn't believe me but my friend convinced them I was from the DRC and that my family were all part of one of the local tribes in my home village of Kabare. They let me go and from that point onwards I knew that I was in danger because my face looked like a Rwandan face.

The wars that continue in the Congo originated in Rwanda. It is a complicated situation but I will try to break it down as simply as possible for the purpose of explaining the dangers that I faced because of my facial features and appearance. The conflict stems from rival tribes wanting the power to lead neighboring Rwanda.

In Rwanda, there are three ethnic groups (tribes) known as the Hutu, the Tutsi and Twa. They are enemies that kill each other through mass genocide in the hope of taking power and leading the country. The long war dates back many decades.

Prior to 1960, a Tutsi tribal leader was the first to govern Rwanda, when still under Belgian colonial rule. The Hutu tribal groups wanted to end Belgian rule, sparking a war of independence during which time there was mass genocide. The Hutu tribe killed many of the Tutsi tribe, causing the Tutsis to flee to neighboring countries and enabling a Hutu president to take power.

The Tutsi soldiers who fled formed rebel groups known as 'inyenzi' and launched unexpected attacks on Rwanda from these neighboring countries. They were successful in their attacks and many different presidents came into power over the years. President Paul Kagame of the Tutsi tribe came into power in Rwanda in 1994. During this time, many of the Hutu soldiers fled their country to the vicinities of Bukavu and Goma in the DRC, living in jungle areas where they amassed great wealth from exploiting Congolese mines.

In my opinion, the Tutsi minority seemed to be organizing and running Rwanda well but they were always concerned that the Hutu tribes could stage unexpected attacks at any time. The Tutsis were determined to locate the Hutu rebel soldiers in the DRC and kill them. They slowly made their way along the river border of the DRC with a powerful Congolese man called Kabila leading them. The Tutsis believed that if they helped Kabila to overthrow President Mobutu of the DRC, it would help them establish their authority in the DRC and enable them to eliminate more Hutu soldiers, known as 'Interahamwe'.

Their plan worked because when they came to the DRC, President Mobutu did not have the ability to fight them and fled the country allowing President Kabila to reign in the DRC. Once Kabila took control, he told the Rwandan Soldiers to leave the DRC. They were furious with Kabila that they couldn't stay to exercise their power as he had promised earlier. The next war began between the Kabila government and the Tutsi groups from Rwanda. This meant that any soldiers from Rwanda that were found by the Congolese soldiers were arrested and/or killed.

Many different wars followed. It is a terribly complicated political situation and one that is difficult to understand without examining it all in entirety. I believe that if the soldiers from Rwanda had been able to go back to their country in peace, the problem in the DRC could have been resolved. That would have involved an extreme level of interjection by the UN and other countries to work together with the hope of finding a peaceful solution to this dreadful situation

Due to this ongoing war and because I looked like a Rwandan, it took me three months to return safely to Bukavu so that I could see my new baby girl. It was such a relief to see them all and in such good health - but I couldn't stay. The war was around us and my safety was at risk. My wife looked like she was from the Congo so she had a little more protection locally but mine was a different case. I asked her to leave with me but she had the newborn baby and our first daughter who was only one year old. She said, "If I die, I die, I can't go". There were around ten million people that died throughout the years as a result of these wars. It was such a dangerous time for everyone.

I had saved some money from my work in Moba and with that money I fled, with the hope that my wife and children would join me later. The city of Bukavu borders Rwanda with the Ruzizi River separating them. There were many people fleeing to escape the war.

The guards could see people running but they couldn't stop us. If I had been a soldier, they would have stopped me to ask where I was going. As for civilians, they let them all pass. I got across the river easily with the help of a local African bamboo raft. When I got to the other side, I used my money to catch a bus through the next border in Cyangugu. On that same day, after six hours on the bus, I reached Kigali, the capital of Rwanda. It was 1999 when I arrived there.

I am an educated man so I worked out fairly quickly what I should do. I met with people from my church congregation and I told them what was happening. They welcomed me in their home to recuperate and I ended up staying with them for six months. It was difficult to be away from my family for so long so I made sure that I sent letters to them through other people, telling them where I was, so that they could eventually join me. In 2000, my wife and daughters arrived in Kigali. My girls had grown so much since I last saw them. It was so good to be reunited with my family again.

I registered with the United Nations and explained my situation. In 2003, I was given refugee status. I was considered a special case because of my different appearance and I fit the criteria for resettlement.

I applied for jobs related to my academic degrees and ended up working as a teacher. I made enough money to support us so I didn't need the help of the United Nations during this time, apart from some medication for the children when they were unwell. We didn't need to live in a refugee camp as I earned enough for us to live in a normal house. I was able to afford our rent and our food and we lived as urban refugees. If I hadn't had a job they would have forced us to go and live in the refugee camps; we were fortunate. There were 72,000 refugees from the Congo living in Rwanda at the time.

My eldest daughter began school and I kept working as a teacher. My wife and I tried to have more children but she had four miscarriages within three years. I kept praying for a baby boy. In Africa there is a belief that it is important to have children of both sexes so that your children are different. Having one sex is never good for a family. My wife became pregnant again and she gave birth to our first baby boy in Kigali. I called him Ashuza, which means 'God responds'. I was so happy to have a son. We went on to have another boy within one year and my last boy seven years later. We have five children in all and I love spending time with them.

My wife spent all her time raising the children whilst I worked. There were only a few schools in our area but I managed to make extra money by teaching at two schools. School was five days a week, and in general, my sons went to primary school in the morning and my daughters went to secondary school in the afternoon. There were not enough classrooms to teach both primary and secondary classes at the same time. I taught at the secondary school. My wife was wonderful and would have our meals ready for us. We enjoyed our family meals together and it reminded me of my time with my mother when we were in the Congo.

I continued to apply through the United Nations to come to Canada. Even though we were settled at the time the groups living outside Rwanda were always looking for ways to destabilize the government in Rwanda. The situation for us could change at any time and so, in the safety of our home, we still lived in fear.

In 2012, I received a call from my brother telling me that my mother had died. Within one day, she fell ill and died. She was 82 years old. It was difficult being far away from her and I cried very much when I heard this sad news. We mourned her death in our home and I eventually came to terms with what had happened.

My faith does not believe in praying for the deceased as the person has now passed on. We must pray whilst we are alive so that God is with us and can intervene in our lives here and now. I believe in resurrection. After our resurrection, we have another life on earth. It is our continued faith in God that will fix the problems in the world. Politicians cannot bring love and peace into the world as they have political interests. The peace will be come through God and not by mankind. I believe we can live in a peaceful world and I believe this will happen.

We were finally advised that we had been accepted to come to Canada. The night before our departure, my son Ashuza told me that he had dreamed of being on a plane for the first time. He was so excited. The whole family was enthused about our new life of better opportunities and good health care. This move for us meant we were coming to a place of peace where I wouldn't feel ridiculed because of my appearance or liable to be attacked with a weapon. My children would have a better future.

We arrived in Canada in December 2013 and began working on our integration. My older children were enrolled in school and are doing well. My youngest boy will go to school next year. I am hopeful that I will find a job in my field soon. Our life here is so much better. My children began to learn French in Africa so that they could speak French and communicate more easily upon our arrival. The system is different but they are adapting well.

I am a product of my prayers and I pray for what I want to be. As a young child I made a decision to never drink, smoke or have affairs. I wanted to be a family man who is kind and loving to his wife and a very good father to his family. I avoid anything that could distract me from being the person who I am. I provide constant advice to my children, help them with their homework and I try to understand their problems and needs.

We do not have much money at the moment and any initial funds that we received from the government for our migration have gone to pay for our rent, phone bills and setting up the phone / internet service and our food. We have heard that the electricity bills are very expensive so I am not looking forward to receiving that bill. The children have very few clothes and there isn't much left over for the girls to buy clothes or to get their own computers. We have faith that, with time, I will be able to find work so that I can provide a better lifestyle for my family. My children want a car because it has been snowing ever since we arrived. Without a car, they have to walk everywhere and freeze - but they will survive and must remain patient meanwhile.

It would be nice to visit our family back in the Congo once the situation settles and maybe, one day when I am rich, the rest of my family could join us. I would love to find work within a humanitarian network so that I can use my experiences to help others. I would love to offer people the same help that I was given.

34

My first daughter wants to be a medical doctor, the other wants to study computer science. My eldest son, Ashuza wants to be a pilot and my second son wants to be an architect. The youngest is too small to know what he wants. I am proud of the family that we have raised and I look forward to our future in Canada.

Chapter III

Refugee story from Colombia

My name is Jaime and I was born in July, 1977 in the Santander Department of Colombia, South America.

I have one brother whom I will call Luis for security reasons. He may still be alive and living in one of the very dangerous and violent zones in Colombia. I do not know where he is or if I will ever see him again. We cannot even try to make contact for security reasons. The rest of my family is all gone and this is my story.

My mother gave birth to four children in our country home. Luis was the oldest, followed by Bernardo, then my sister Alyssia and I was born last, the baby of the family. We siblings were all very close and loved each other very much.

As hospitals are not easily accessible due to their distance from rural areas, most country births occur at home. Birth certificates are not generally issued unless government officials call at your home for some reason and record the new birth. Often, the date of birth is estimated. This is slowly changing as villages grow and births are recorded more frequently. My parents didn't have papers as the system was not in place at the time. It is hard to establish the ages of elderly people living in villages for this very reason. There are still no churches, municipality offices, hospitals or many facilities in these areas.

I will try to explain the political situation in Colombia so that you may understand my story completely.

The rural areas of Colombia are very dangerous because guerilla groups hide in the jungle areas in preparation for retaliation against government forces. Santander is such a rural area with many mountains, small villages, farmlands and jungle. We are permitted to move between villages but we must always remain in the same department.

There was, and still is, a huge corruption issue within the government of Colombia. People had no jobs, there was exploitation of many people who were forced to work for big companies mining for gold and coal and got paid very little, if anything, and the general population did not receive any help from the government. If people cannot work to make money, and there is no help from the government, the people suffer and everything deteriorates. When people suffer, they form groups to retaliate against their oppressors.

The government sent a huge army force into the countryside to take over peoples' properties so that the government could acquire more land. Everything can change within five minutes of these groups forcing their way into the village areas. The army uses the paramilitary groups to do their dirty work for them. Paramilitary groups are like soldiers that train in their own camps and are utilized by the government forces, as well as the influential drug traffickers, to do their dirty work. Depending on who demands their services, depends on what uniform they don. They can wear the army uniform, plain civilian clothes or their training camp outfits. When they work for the government, they wear soldier-like clothing with the army logo at the front and on their sleeves they have a round black and white emblem with the words SAUSAE engraved in it, which means they are there to defend the people. They are similar to military police. They float around waiting to get their next job from government forces or drug lords. They use tactics to scare people to make sure no villages form an alliance against the government.

The Drug lords send the corrupt army, paramilitary or drug lords themselves into the villages to take over farming land so that they can use it to grow the coca plant used to make the drug Cocaine. Only a few people that have a connection with one of the army or paramilitary groups can stay and work to crop the drug plantation. All others have to leave and give up their land. If anyone tries to answer back or question their actions they are tortured and killed. If anyone is seen to protest or place signs up in the areas or in their homes, they are killed. The paramilitary are sent to the villages to see if people are causing trouble for them by voicing their opinions. They go into the villages and torture people randomly to try and get information about anyone who could be causing trouble. It is a terrible, terrible situation for the average person.

Paramilitary groups are allocated jobs according to a hierarchical system. The darker the skin color, the worse the job one is assigned to carry out against the village people. Generally, black people, Indian people and some of mixed races are made to perform the lowest ranking jobs. That is why anyone in a position of authority in these armed forces is mostly white.

Due to this repression by government forces and drug lords, people grow tired of having no rights and having their land taken from them. In order to survive, they freely and willingly form groups to feel protected by an alliance. They join a group, learn how to use weapons and fight. These guerilla groups expand in force and they hide in the mountain areas within the jungle and wait for their next move and attack.

There is an ongoing war between these guerilla groups and the corrupt government forces. Two of the biggest guerilla groups are FARC and ELN. The biggest group with approximately 8,000 to 13,000 members is FARC (Revolutionary Armed Forces of Colombia) referred to as the People's Army which formed in 1964. The ELN group (National Liberation Army of Colombia) have a few thousand members and are mainly known to hide out in the jungles. Both groups have been classified as terrorist organizations by Colombia, the USA and many other countries.

Ordinary, hard-working people are caught up in the middle of this conflict. If they are captured by guerilla groups and found to be siding with government forces, they are killed. If they are deemed to be siding with guerilla groups, they are killed by the paramilitary. There is no way out. People live in fear as members of any of these groups can enter a village unexpectedly to threaten and instill fear in the community so that people stay quiet. Everyone is always in danger.

In a nutshell, the main problems in Colombia are the corrupt government and the power wielded by the drug lords.

My family all lived together in our home and we lived in the constant fear of hostility. We were a quiet, humble family that just wanted to live peacefully and not have anything to do with any of these groups. I farmed the land with my father and brother Bernardo. My sister Alyssia worked for a church group and did humanitarian work to help people in the country. Her boyfriend and their young child lived with us. My oldest brother Luis, his wife and children were also with us – the family was growing.

When I was eight years old in 1985, my parents decided to move to another village in the same department. The siblings, who were much older than me, stayed in the house whilst I left with my parents.

We settled in a house at the edge of a jungle. The land was approximately 37,000 square meters. It was a very densely wooded area so it is not a typical farm that one would find in other open areas. We had many crops on our land such as coffee, chocolate, cocoa and the edible root yuka (yuca), a major source of carbohydrate and a Colombian staple.

These farms are known as "fincas". Our house was wooden with a roof made of palm tree leaves which stopped water from penetrating and rotting the internal timber. There is no electricity or running water in jungle areas. Water is collected from the river. Most people who work in fincas wear farm boots and carry a big machete which is used for protection as well as for harvesting the coffee crops. Machetes are also used to cut through vegetation and make a walking trail.

There was a local school nearby which was also used as a church on Sunday mornings where villagers could pray and where children could play together afterwards. If we ever needed to catch a bus anywhere, we would walk 2-3 hours along narrow dirt paths in the mountainous jungle area to the main dirt road where we would be picked up and dropped off by the bus.

During the first three years at the finca, my brothers and sister would visit often with their children. When I turned eleven, my brother Bernardo and my sister suddenly disappeared.

The paramilitary came to their house and took Alyssia and her son - we never saw them again. Alyssia was 22 years old at the time.

Bernardo was taken soon afterwards and also never returned. He was 28 years old. We tried to look for them but the authorities were never any help. After Alyssia and Bernardo went missing, Luis visited us a few times to tell us what had happened in the village. After that, he also disappeared and I haven't seen him since.

I would love to find my brothers, my sister and her little boy but it is hard to imagine that they haven't been killed and thrown into the river. Many people were taken from their homes and tortured for information, or in my sisters' case, she was punished for helping people through her humanitarian work. Some people were forced to work at detention centers during their construction. Once the work was finished, they were cut up into pieces and thrown into the river so that they couldn't tell anyone about what was happening or who was doing the killing. It is extremely painful and very frightening to think of what could have happened to my siblings. I have a deep sadness within me. It is 25 years since I last saw them.

After their disappearance, my parents and I kept managing the crops on our land, going to church on Sundays and doing the best we could to continue living through the loss of my siblings.

When I had just turned 16 in 1994, one Sunday morning my parents and I went to church and afterwards, I played soccer with the local village kids. Sunday is the only day that we were not allowed to wear our boots or take our machetes with us so we all wore simple clothing like jeans and sneakers.

When we arrived home, I helped my parents prepare our lunch. We were cooking yuka to accompany 'asado de carne', a dish made with meat and a rich sauce.

At about 10am, whilst we were preparing the food, paramilitary groups suddenly barged into our house, baring their weapons and forcing us outside. They ordered us to walk to the school soccer field immediately. My parents and I knew not to say anything and to do as they asked so that we were not killed on the spot. We learnt to obey at all costs. All in our and the neighboring villages were approached at the same time and sent to the school field. The army waited outside the village and watched to ensure that the paramilitary did their job correctly.

There were approximately 50 villagers and between 85 to 100 people in total in the field. The paramilitary all wore their military outfits with the black and white emblem and held guns in their hands. People were made to stand in a group in the middle of the field. Soldiers were interspersed between them.

The villagers had fear in their eyes, unsure of what was going to happen next. I stood standing with my parents towards the back of the group. The soldiers pointed out three people randomly and told them to come to the front. The first was a young local village boy who was mute, the second was a 59 year old local village man called Pedro and the third was a man from a neighboring village who was passing through the area.

Their arms were tied up and they were placed in the center of the group so that everyone could see them. The darkest skinned soldier stood in front of them. He was clearly the lowest ranked paramilitary member there. We watched him inject himself with drugs, probably such as heroin to be able to cope with what he was about to do. Many soldiers became drug addicts because it is the only way that they could cope with carrying out their duties.

Once he shot up, he began yelling at the mute boy, demanding answers to his questions. The poor boy couldn't reply because he couldn't speak. No one could say anything in his defense or they would be killed instantly.

As he continued to question the boy, the soldier picked up a chainsaw and started it. The villagers were terrified. The look on the boy's face was something that we will never forget. The soldier then sawed through the boy's right ankle until it fell off. There was a terrified look on the boy's face and he couldn't utter a sound. We could see the pain in his eyes.

People in the crowd were screaming. Some fainted on the spot. The soldier stopped yelling and kept sawing each part of the boy's body from the right side across the body, all the way to the head. They use the same method for mutilations. They are trained to carry out the killings in the same sequence.

When they finished cutting up the first boy, I began vomiting. I did not want to watch this horrendous mutilation. Like everyone else, I wanted to stop it but we were powerless and outnumbered.

They began cutting Pedro, our village friend, starting from the right side. His intense and penetrating screams pierced through each of us standing there; my mother fainted. My father and I caught her just before she hit the ground and used that brief moment to avert our eyes from the horrendous scene that we were forced to watch. People started screaming and wailing and many passed out around us.

Others had their hands in front of their eyes so they wouldn't be able to see any more. The soldiers moved along the front line of the group and pushed their hands away, forcing them to watch. I was in a total state of shock, disbelief and confusion by the time the third man was murdered. When they finished with him, we were given three minutes to leave the area and disappear into the bush. Everyone was extremely traumatized and in a deep state of fear, shock and sorrow.

This was the first time that I saw this happen in our village. My parents, however, had witnessed similar atrocities at our previous village. The most difficult part for us to cope with, apart from the psychological effects and the nightmares, was knowing that we were powerless to do anything. Village people are farmers, peaceful people who want no quarrels. They hunt for food with machetes and only a few of them have ever used firearms to hunt. They never use these weapons against other human beings. I cannot believe how these soldiers killed these innocent farmers with such ease. We are all people living our lives together on this earth. It was horrific in every sense of the word.

We ran into the jungle immediately and at night we returned to our house to fetch what we needed to survive in the jungle. We could not stop crying. My parents and I prayed continuously as that was our only source of consolation.

Two days later, when I ran back to the village, I saw that the bodies were still there. I felt that I needed to do something so I gathered three other people from our village and together we went to a neighboring village to find one of the catholic fathers at the church. We wanted to tell him what had happened so that somebody could witness the incident. The priest came to the village and we asked him to report the incident and lodge a complaint about what happened. He explained to us that when complaints are made, no one actually knows what action, if any, is taken. He said he would do it for us. A day or two later, civil defense members came to remove the bodies.

When someone from the church collects the bodies, they conduct a funeral and bury them. In the past when such incidents occurred, priests attempted to provide pastoral and psychological help to the villagers. It happens more rarely now because of the danger associated with helping people. If a village is seen to be getting help, neighboring villages will ask questions as to what happened and why they are getting help. The various military groups make it clear by their tactics that they do not wish for anyone to find out about what happened or which group is responsible. If guerilla groups know there are witnesses to government endorsed killings, they can go in and interrogate people to find out what they saw and who was responsible so that they can retaliate. It is extremely dangerous for any villager to help or provide information to anyone. It is a terrible cycle with village people always caught in the middle of it.

I kept praying to God to help me accept what had happened so that I could cope with the damaging psychological effect that this terrible event had on me. In spite of my prayers, I developed a deep sense of anger and hatred. It continued to gnaw at me. I felt so helpless but I knew I needed to help myself to move on and heal the aggression burning inside me. My prayers and enduring faith in God provided me with the psychological support that I needed.

After that horrific incident, we hid in the jungle for one month and then decided to head for a village called Barranca for about fifteen days. We then came back to our village to see if there were any soldiers around and when it seemed that they had moved on, we came back and worked on our land.

The paramilitary came in and out of the village for the next ten months to check on what was happening with the people but nothing happened abnormal happened until 1995, less than one year after the massacres. I was still sixteen at the time.

It was 12pm and my parents and I were in the dining area of our house. Paramilitary soldiers barged in and I heard one of the soldiers call his leader Roqui. He forced me outside. My parents warily tried to stop them from taking me so they shut my parents in the other room. They were told not to do or say anything.

The soldiers accused me of helping one of the guerilla groups. Our family was part of a church group and because we helped people with food, they were accusing us of giving food to a guerilla group. This was not true. They used these types of tactics to scare us and force us to say things that were not true. If we were accused of being against the government forces and the drug lords, they had an excuse to take over our land for drug plantations. The paramilitary were sent to each house at the same time on this particular day. They randomly selected one member in each family and applied the same torture to each person.

A man called Carlos, an extremely well known drug lord in Colombia, was behind these attacks. People were told to either stay and work the land or leave. These wealthy drug lords have so much power in Colombia that the government groups close their eyes to the problem. The paramilitary are paid by Carlos to go in and do the dirty work to get our land.

Roqui tied my hands behind my back and threw me to the ground. There were about five paramilitary soldiers and they used their batons to beat me all over my body. They used the butt of a gun to strike the back of my head several times. One of the baton strikes was so hard that I lost movement and sensation on both sides of my ears and the back of my head.

One of the soldiers began to push thorns that they get from a local tree under my toe nails. This is a common tactic used to get people to talk as it is very painful. I had nothing to say. I hadn't done anything.

All five soldiers were torturing me at the same time. They poured extremely salty water down my nose and ears. They placed a cloth over my mouth so that I was forced to swallow what was put in my mouth. They did that until I fainted.

They kept beating me until my body was completely covered in bruises and gashes and the thorns pierced the flesh under my toenails. The pain was excruciating and my body was black. They dragged me deeper into the jungle and left me there, thinking that I would die shortly afterwards. I couldn't move any part of my body. As the night settled in, mosquitos and small insects began to feed on my open wounds. Nighttime is quite cool in the jungle whilst daytime is quite warm. If it rains, the weather at night gets a lot colder.

By the morning, I had a terrible fever and I was moving in and out of consciousness. The insect bites were increasingly painful. I laid there helpless and all I had was my faith in God and I clung onto my faith the entire time that I was there. It was a miracle that I was still alive. With every minute that passed, my wounds were becoming more infected and the paralysis was worsening.

On the third morning, my father finally found me after searching for me with some other men from our village. It was my father's faith and instinct that convinced him that I was still alive out there, somewhere. I was in excruciating pain but the feeling that overcame me when my father found me was undeniably that of deepest love that I have ever felt towards him. It was a miracle that they found me. My father cried tears of sorrow and joy when he found his baby boy alive.

They immediately made a stretcher from jungle vines and plants and carried me for one and a half days through the jungle to the closest village hospital. I was there for one day but they didn't have the resources needed to attend to me. We couldn't leave the hospital by vehicle because the paramilitary was checking identity papers.

The men had to carry me on a stretcher through the jungle and around a mountain to get me to a bigger hospital. It was so difficult for them to carry me all that way through the rugged terrain. The four men who came with my father were heroic angels to help us the way that they did, risking their lives to help my father and his son. It was a beautiful act of love and support by local villagers – this is the type of people that they are.

When we arrived at the hospital the Red Cross were there to help me and they paid for my stay at the hospital and all my medication. My left ear was so badly infected that gangrene had started setting in. My left ear does not function anymore and my right ear only has approximately 60% of hearing remaining and that is slowly deteriorating.

There was a priest at the hospital who was a rights activist and he compiled a written complaint about my case and sent it to the U.N. Human Rights Commission and the High Commission of Colombia. After lodging the complaint, the priest was informed that I would be in danger for making such a complaint and I would need to get out of the department where I lived so that I wouldn't be found and killed.

I was at the hospital for fifteen days. When we got back to the village, we had to leave immediately. The priest organized for my parents and me to be hidden in a car and driven away from the village.

The priest not only organized our escape but also gave us money to pay for all the transport along the way. He had saved a little money from church services to help people like me escape. We were put on a long distance bus. A nurse from Switzerland accompanied us and stayed by me the entire trip to provide any medical assistance that I required. The bus journey took 52 hours, which was three days of travelling with frequent stops along the way. We were fed at secret humanitarian places that were set up along the way and I remember one of the German nurses, Nicole who helped treat me at one of the stops. There are organizations that have been established to help people in extreme danger get across borders. These people are immensely brave to do what they do for their fellow human beings.

The journey was difficult for me both physically and emotionally. I was in constant pain but the fear and worry about what was happening to my family and where we would end up was plaguing me and torturing my mind with thoughts about all that had happened. We finally arrived in southern Colombia and settled in a region that was totally new to us. It was a lot quieter and people were not being killed. Whilst I was recovering from my wounds, my parents received a small piece of land for them to work. It took me a long time to heal and once I was able to move, I helped my father on our land.

A few years later in 1998, when I was much improved health-wise, I met a woman from the region and we were married. She came to live with us in our home.

A year after we married, the priest sent me a message to alert me that the situation was about to turn bad for us. He had prepared a special written letter for us to carry and stressed that we needed to leave immediately.

In mid 1999 we all left by bus for Ecuador. I gave the letter to the authorities in Quito, Ecuador which entitled us to meet with the United Nations High Commission for refugees (UNHCR). With these papers, we were granted refugee status and permitted to remain in Ecuador as refugees.

It is difficult being a refugee because people treat you like an outcast. No-one wants you to have the same equal rights because you are not from their country.

We rented a small home in Ecuador. There was no refugee camp so we lived in a normal local house. My wife fell pregnant soon after we settled in Ecuador and gave birth to our first son in 2000. It was such a joy to have our new baby who represented the start of a new life for us all and helped us move on from the pain of the past. As refugees, it wasn't easy for us to raise our baby but it was a lot safer for us to be there as a family than in our former villages. Two months after our baby's birth, my father got sick and died. I was with him at the time of his death and it was a very difficult time. It was tough on my mother who, after experiencing such heartache in her life, now lost her husband.

We met other Colombians in Ecuador and we tended to socialize with them as they were all in similar situations and we supported one another. We had our second child in Ecuador and that was a blessing for us as a family.

My mother eventually left to go back to Colombia in 2011. It was too dangerous for me to go back with her. She was getting older and she said she wanted to die in her own country. All the travelling, the grief and the pain in her life affected her state of mind deeply. I tried to relate to how hard it was for her emotionally to have suffered the way she did from the loss of her family over the years.

In January 2012, I received a call from the priest, informing me that my mother had died of natural causes. I knew it was her time to pass. She was filled with such deep sorrow.

After her death, I continued filing complaints about what happened to me and my family. The filing of these complaints caused me ongoing problems and gave me a sense of insecurity. The priest contacted me again and told me that if I kept filing complaints, soldiers would be sent to Ecuador to kill me. I took that letter to the United Nations. They made two application requests to get us out of the country to either Switzerland or Canada. Canada processed the request faster and we were flown out within a few months on Air Canada.

I was very emotional on the plane because I had never thought for one moment that we would ever be able to leave Ecuador. I was so happy that we were going to a country that would be safer for my family. I knew it was not going to be paradise as a refugee in another country and I would need to overcome some challenges but we were happy.

The tranquility in Canada and the sense of freedom to go anywhere that we want is such a blessing for me. I am studying French for a second year so that I can communicate more effectively. It is hard to be 37 years old and not to have had any education. I have disabilities and limitations with my hearing due to the torture and I have no feeling in my right hand. But we are safe and for that I am grateful.

When I look back at my life, I think about what I went through and try to remain calm so that the anger, hurt and emotional pain can be controlled. I miss my parents, my brother Luis who is somewhere out there and I think about my missing brother Bernardo and my sister Alyssia often.

It would be a blessing to have a proper home for my family like we had in Colombia before it was stripped away from us. We don't have a car which makes it really hard in the winter to get around with small children as we have to walk everywhere, even when it is snowing.

Since being here, I have filed all my complaints as one combined case and I am trying to fight through the corruption in my home country. I know it is dangerous for me to tell my story but someone needs to be brave enough to stand up and tell the world what is happening to the local village people in Colombia who are trapped with no safe place to go. They are beautiful people who are loving, kind, caring and compassionate, just like the men who carried me on a stretcher for days without a word of complaint.

I would like to end my story by extending my deepest gratitude to the priest who helped my family escape to a place of safety: I want to say thank you for all your support and hard work. These remarkable priests are religious people who are part of the Christian community of justice and peace. They are part of a Not for Profit Organization and they do the most amazing work for people in need. They put their lives on the line for others and spread the message of love for all mankind in this way. They live with integrity and do not accept corruption or the exploitation of people. They are brave souls and earthly angels sent here to give us hope that faith in God and love for humanity is at the core of healing our troubled country.

Chapter IV

Refugee from Kosovo

I was given a traditional name by my parents at birth but I now prefer to go by the name Ariana. I was born in southern Kosovo in June 1988 in a hospital in Ferizaj, about 25 kms from our family home in Kačanik. Kosovo is a landlocked south-eastern European country which has borders with Montenegro, Serbia, Macedonia and Albania. Kosovo was the poorest region of the former Socialist Federal Republic of Yugoslavia, which dissolved in 1991 due to a rise of nationalism.

There were six in our immediate family: I had a sister who was two years older than me and two younger brothers born in 1992 and 1995 respectively. We were a very close-knit family; the siblings all got on well together. My sister and I were very protective of our brothers and always looked out for them. We must have taken after my mother as she was also very protective of us when we were little. My mother was the stricter parent. When wanting to stay up later at night, I remember running to my father rather than my mother. My father is a really cool guy and he would always give in to us and negotiate with my mother to give us a little more time. As an adult, I can understand more why my mother was so strict with us. She always taught us to respect our elders, never hurt anyone and never steal. I have had a good relationship with both of my parents over the years.

My family lived in a grand, solid four bedroom concrete house. Growing up, we had everything we needed. We were a middle class family and always had boots for winter and everything we needed to live comfortably. We all started school when we reached the age of five. An uncle and his family lived next door to us, my grandparents lived with one of my other uncles. There were no nursing homes back then so it was easier for my grandparents to live with my uncle. We all spent a lot of time together. My grandfather died four years ago and my grandmother is still alive and in good condition at 87 years of age.

In 1992, when I was around five years old, a war broke out to the north of Kosovo between Serbia and Bosnia. It didn't affect us where we lived but we heard of people being killed in these countries. It was a war of independence as Bosnia wanted to become an independent country and separate from Serbia.

By 1998, another war of independence started between Kosovo and Serbia. It was an economic war as Serbia wanted to keep Kosovo, formerly an autonomous part of Serbia, but Kosovo wanted its independence.

I was in the 5th grade at school when things got very bad. Reports were televised constantly and soon it was announced that schools were to close down for the safety of the students. We spent every day at home as it was unsafe to go anywhere. When people left their homes to drive anywhere, the Serbian army would stop them, questioning them about where they were going and what they were doing. If they didn't like their response, they would kill them. Many people protested in the streets against the Serbians taking over their country. As soon as the protests began, the army used force to push back the protestors. If the protestors resisted, the army started shooting. Many protestors were killed.

My parents explained to us what was happening and tried to encourage us to remain calm and not be afraid of what was being reported. When we heard the planes overhead or gun shots in the vicinity, my parents would try to hide the truth and say that it meant nothing and that it would go away.

The US and UK armies intervened to help us retaliate against the force of the Serbian Army. They tried to negotiate to a certain point and warned the Serbian Government that if they didn't take their troops out of the country, they would start to shoot. Everyone was told on the news about the situation and that the shooting was about to begin. The Serbian Army remained in place and became even more forceful and aggressive.

I remember that day. I was ten years old and it was night time. The entire family was in our living room, including my uncles, cousins and grandparents. We were all watching the television broadcast to know what was happening and waiting to see if the US and UK army would start to shoot.

The shooting began as scheduled and it was loud and all the kids started screaming and yelling. I remember my brother's face because he was crying from such intense fear. My grandfather spoke with my parents and uncles and they decided to make a plan for us. We knew the foreign armies were there to help the country with its independence struggle but the people of Kosovo were still living inside their homes whilst the Serbian Army was on the streets. It was a dangerous time.

Our family, neighbors and every one we knew assembled together - there were 35 kids in total. Behind our house was a back gate so we all walked through the gate and along the river bank until we got to the forest which was a five minute walk away. They thought if we got out of our homes and into the shelter of the forest, we may have a better chance of survival during the shooting.

It was a cold night and we stayed in the forest all night. Everyone was sitting on pieces of wood and I remember my mother had a bag of water with some bread and cookies. Our neighbors' daughter thought everybody was playing a big game of hide and seek and she was saying "I see you" so my grandmother nursed her on her knees and put her hand on her mouth telling her to "Shhh" to quieten her down.

My older sister and I were leaning on our mother's shoulders, trying to sleep. My dad was looking after my brothers and cousin and all the uncles and my grandparents shared the responsibility of protecting all the children. No one wanted to attract attention to us so it was crucial that everyone remained quiet.

By 5am in the morning, we were getting very cold and my grandmother suggested that we stay together and walk back to the house so we could get more food and clean ourselves. It was a good idea. When we got back, my grandmother started cooking for all of us on the outside stove. It was simple food like bread and rice. My mother changed all our dirty clothes and bathed my baby brother. She put us into our beds that night and we slept well.

We heard on the news that all the trains had stopped but at 8am the following morning, my mother saw a train going south. By midday she told my dad we should take the train. My grandmother disagreed because she would not know where we were but my mother explained that it would be safer if we separated rather than staying together.

All my six uncles from dad's side of the family decided to stay with my grandparents. My parents took their children and two of our neighbors' children with them. We boarded a train and it took us to Macedonia. Everyone was standing in the train because it was so full of people. I remember that my neighbor gave his seat to a pregnant lady and I thought that was a really beautiful thing to do. After we were on the train for about one hour, I looked out the window and could see a thick cloud of smoke coming from houses. The train had travelled through a mountain pass and as it exited, a view of a town appeared. The whole area was lit up with flames and smoke was pouring from houses. I kept asking my parents why they were burning the houses and even though they tried to explain it to us, I still couldn't understand why.

When we arrived in Macedonia, many Albanians were living there. An Albanian man that I didn't know came to meet us and take us to his home. The man was around fifty years of age, tall and skinny with a long moustache. He was with his brother and they each took a family with them. He had an SUV and we squeezed into his car until we got to a big house with a huge balcony. His wife was waiting for us out the front and she hugged each of us and asked us if we were hungry.

We were taken inside, shown around the house, taken to our rooms so that we knew where we would to sleep and shower and then we were offered drinks. My mother was given a key to the house and I remember that first night, whilst drinking tea and eating a really big cookie, that I felt safe and happy. My little brother stayed with my parents in their room. My other brother became friends with the owners' sons and they all played together and ended up sleeping in the same bedroom. My sister and I shared a room with their two daughters.

My mother made us go to the local school and we begged not to go because we didn't know anyone. It was quite a bizarre experience and so different to what we were used to. We managed to understand everyone at school because we spoke Albanian and they spoke both Albanian and Macedonian. Within three weeks, we had made friends at school and were feeling a lot better.

At that time, my father heard that a lot of countries in Europe were taking refugees from the war. He knew that if we went there, it would only be a temporary solution and it was possible that, within a few years, they would make us leave their country. My father made some more enquiries at one of the offices in town. He did not want to inconvenience this family anymore as we had already been there for three weeks. My father asked the man if he could take us to the local refugee camp which the man did. Once we said our goodbyes, we never saw that family again.

I could see a big fence around a huge piece of land, with a big white tent located inside. There were many more of these tents located on the terrain. It was a big camp and before you entered, there was someone at the gate taking family names and details. Once a tent was cleaned and cleared, they took you to the tent to set up. They gave us blankets, food, water and we were told that we had to share the bathrooms. There were separate showers for men and women and the line was always very long. My mother took us for a walk around the camp site where we saw other people in their tents and looked for people from our city.

We stayed in those conditions for one week and by the end of that week, we were all crying, wanting our beds back at home. I realize now how hard it was for my parents, especially my mother. My brother and sister were still very young and my mother had to give my brother his milk. My dad left often to read the big blackboard they had set up with documents displayed. Each form represented a different country. He chose Canada and put his name on the sheet. Two days later, we were on a plane for Ontario. My father told us that he chose a country as far away as possible and that he had always wanted to come to Canada for a holiday.

It was my first time on a plane and I remember how big the plane was. My dad was sitting with my two brothers and my mum was sitting with my sister and me. My mum was crying on the plane. She had left her entire family behind for the safety of her children. At one point on the flight, I looked out the window and pointed. I said to my mum, "Look mama, it's another plane. We are not alone".

The flight took eight hours and we kept getting up and walking around the plane. We arrived in Canada in May of 1999 and one month later it would be my birthday.

We landed in Kingston, Ontario and stayed at the Canadian Military Camp. They had three big buildings set up. It looked like a hospital from the outside and we were allocated three rooms. It was full of other families.

We ate in a separate building that was set up like a big reception center. Our meals were buffet-style.

The children were entertained and offered different activities. They tried to cheer us all up because so many of the children were upset and crying all the time because they had left their homes and families. One day they put on a big aircraft show in the sky. I really loved it and I stood there wandering how they flew in time together. On another day they took us for a picnic at the local boat marina. After dinner, we played games and participated in various activities. At times we tried to play volleyball inside, near our parents, but they yelled at us to go outside and play.

Two of my uncles joined us after two weeks of our being in that camp and we were so excited that they had found us. My uncle in Switzerland had got a message to them when we were in Macedonia, stating that we were at the refugee camp and hopefully heading for Canada. They also chose Canada to be with us. It was so good to see and play with my eight cousins again.

One day, after spending one month at the military camp, we saw our family name on a paper stating that we were heading to St Jérome in Quebec. They put us on a bus to a hotel near the airport at Mirabel. We stayed there for two days until the local center (the Coffret) organized to take us to our address. They put us on a yellow bus and transported us to our apartment. When we got inside, we saw it was furnished with all the basic necessities. We were so excited to have a new home and sad at the same time with what we had been forced to give up.

Each family was given a local Quebec family to show them around and to explain how systems work in the area. None of us spoke French or English so it was very difficult initially. We looked at the family with blank faces when they tried to talk to us. We would look at our mum and she couldn't understand them either.

After three months, my mum asked if we could move because we were all only speaking Albanian with each other and all our neighbors and she wanted us to move to a different place in St Jérome so that we could speak French with French people and learn French a lot faster.

We started our studies at the local school. It was a really tough change as we had no school uniforms at the time and we didn't have many clothes.

All of us went to school, except for my baby brother. A lady came to take us to school. She was a language teacher at the school and she tried teaching us the French alphabet and language. As we were all together and placed in a class with other Albanian children, we laughed all the time and made her mad. She decided to separate us and that was much better. I started my 5th grade again.

Within one week, they found us another apartment, as my mother had requested, so we moved and changed schools again. I liked this school better because it was nicer and we made friends quickly with some of the local kids who were our age. They were our new friends and we were happy.

I am so glad that we came to Canada. We have now been here for fifteen years. I managed to save enough money to visit Kosovo almost every year. When the war ended, my parents kept their house and never rented it. My aunty cleans and maintains the house. I go to our old house and then spend the rest of the time at my uncles' houses visiting all. Now that we are older, my parents go back so they can visit their family.

I love it here. Apart from the cold, it's great. I have finished my secondary education and now I want to go to university. I have a good job and my sister and I bought a house together seven years ago when I was 17. I started working when I was very young. I met some people on a bus and asked them what they were doing. They said they were picking strawberries. It was tough work but I went and made my money.

We were lucky to leave Kosovo when we did because my parents told us that the army was going into peoples' houses and killing them. No one in our family was killed because we didn't stay long enough for that to happen. It was good that we left when we did.

Looking back over everything now, I feel that it was a stupid, pointless war. The Serbian army killed innocent people, even pregnant women and their unborn babies, to take a country for themselves. The war has ended now but the Serbians are still bitter towards the people of Kosovo for winning the war of independence and separating the two countries.

Chapter V

Refugee from Bhutan in Nepal

My name is Nandu and I was born on the 21st June 1977 in Tsirang District in the southern part of Bhutan. I don't have a birth certificate as my mother gave birth to me in the house on our family farm. This was common practice for people in Bhutan as the hospital was very far away. I was the fourth child to be born in our household after my two older brothers, Narapati and Tika Ram and my sister, Padma.

When I was about 6 months old, we moved further south to a town called Sarpang. My father wanted to be closer to the Indian border in order to do more business in the urban areas, something that was difficult to do when one lived far away in a rural area.

I grew up in Sarpang and it was here that my mother gave birth to my younger sister Maya, and my two younger brothers Narayan and Som. There were now seven children in our family.

My parents were busy doing the farming, growing rice in the fields and then selling our vegetables and rice. My older brothers helped on the farm. The money they made from agriculture was used for food and other necessities. My father would leave to go to the town store and get anything else we needed whilst my mother looked after us and cooked for her large family.

When I was 13 my father's friend spoke with my father by phone about a girl from another family in a village far away. They arranged for my older brother Narapati to meet her with the prospect of marriage. My father and brother set off for the village, 500km away. My brother spent some time with the girl and a date was set for the wedding. Everyone from our village as well as the bride's family came to our house for the wedding. There were over 50 people there and all enjoyed this very special occasion. It was a wonderful day with many different types of food, dancing and celebration. The newlyweds continued to live with us as our house was big enough for all and there was enough land to grow most of our food. It wasn't long before my brother and his wife had their first child.

At 6 years of age, I started primary school. I liked school and the teachers very much. The teachers were from Kerala, southern India. The Bhutan government recruited them to teach us as they were considered to be well educated.

I was in 6th grade and had just completed the half yearly test when the aggression led by the army started in the western part of Bhutan. The king had ordered that any persons living in Bhutan, who were not Bhutanese, were to leave the country. Furthermore, no-one was allowed to speak or be taught in Nepali.

We were not even aware that this was happening at the time that it began. We were studying a subject in our mother language, Nepali when one day some people came and burnt all the books that were from Nepal. After that, the situation at school changed quickly and we were not allowed to study in Nepali anymore. After three to four months, the teachers told us some very distressing news that it was not safe for us to stay at school. The school was closed down and we were told to go home. That day, I walked home quickly with my friends and we were all very afraid. There was a heavy presence of police and army trucks with soldiers brandishing their weapons. Local people from the nearby village were running everywhere in a panicked state. I saw people being arrested and driven away, standing in the back of trucks. My friends and I were terrified by that stage. We were told that they had started killing people in parts of the country. My parents waited anxiously for me to arrive home and when we finally saw each other, we hugged each other in great relief.

None of us went anywhere during this period of upheaval and after two to three months we saw the army and police visit our neighbors' house. We stayed inside our house in the living area, fearing the worst. Soon afterwards, the authorities entered our house and informed us that we had 15 days to leave and that this was no longer our home. They were harsh in their tone, saying, "This is no longer your property"….."You have no right to live here on this land".

My parents decided that we needed to leave as soon as possible. We later learned that some people in our village had decided to stay. The army came through and burnt down all the houses in our village and all the people that did not want to leave were arrested.

I was 15 years old the day that we left our home so I remember everything. There were ten of us altogether, eight children and my parents. We walked across the border into Assam, India. We stayed at our relatives' house for one week. It took that long to organize a bus to Nepal. My father had brought some money with him and used it to pay for the bus fare. When we got to Nepal, there was nothing organized for all the refugees that were forced to flee so my father went to the local village to rent a house for us. He wasn't allowed to work and by the end of 1991 we ran out of the money that he had brought with him. We heard that there were a few facilities in place and we had no choice but to go to the temporary refugee shelter that was set up near the river in Nepal. The temporary camp shelter was called Maidhar Camp.

Our new location was a horrific experience and shock to all of us. We were given a piece of plastic and some wood to make a shelter. We had no clothes, no blankets and hardly any food. The facility was right near the dry bank of the river so in the summer months the dust would come up and blow through the shelter, tearing everything down.

The strong winds blew the dust particles into every crevice in our bodies and throughout our few possessions. Many people got terribly sick and there was a bacterial disease that spread quickly amongst the people causing blood in the stool. There were not enough medical facilities to treat the disease and many people died. The condition stemmed from bacteria in the water.

There were no toilet facilities and people relieved themselves anywhere that they could. Along the riverbank was a little forest of trees where people would go to the toilet and all this waste seeped into the water. There were at least 3,000 people in this area. We had no choice but to drink the water at the site from the river where people swam and cleaned themselves. We stayed there 6-8 months and it was horrific.

At one time or another, all of my family members had blood in their stool but as our immune systems were strong, we managed to survive. The majority of people that died were young children and elderly people.

When the winds picked up and the rain came pouring down we would have to stay awake all night taking turns to hold down the plastic on our flimsy roof shelter. We hardly slept and by the time morning came we found many more people dead under their shelters from the appalling conditions to which we were subjected to. On many occasions my friends and I would walk around the shelter and count the dead bodies. On one particular day we counted more than 50 dead people. It happened frequently.

In order to get food, we had to line up near a temple which was near the camp entrance. The United Nations officials distributed rice, a few vegetables and some lentils. We would have to fetch wood from the forest, make a fire and cook the food in the pots that we carried from our home in Bhutan. There was never enough food.

After 6 months of living in absolute squalor, the official refugee camp sites were set up and we were sent to camp Beldagi1, one of seven camps. There were approximately 22,000 people in our camp site. I am not exactly sure of the numbers but ours was the second biggest camp site. Our camp was split into 7 different sectors and we were assigned to sector D, sub sector 1 and our huts were numbers 75 and 76. It was a double hut because we were a bigger family. They gave us kerosene oil to use for light and charcoal for cooking but most of the time we found it easier to use firewood. The United Nations aid share unit eventually gave us a better oven to use.

When we first arrived, we were sharing the double hut with my older brother and his wife who by now had three children. When I was 16, my sister Padma found a husband in the same camp but on another sector line so she moved to his hut. They eventually had three children.

It was soon afterwards that my brother Tika Ram got married to a girl in nearby Bedangi 2. Usually when a couple marry, the woman goes to the man's hut but when you had more than 8-9 people in a hut, some could move to another hut. My brother was allowed to separate from us after a few months of being married and get his own hut. This gave us more room and he and his wife started a family and eventually had four children. Our family was expanding rapidly.

Between 1992 and 1995, I attended Grades 7 to 10 at the camp school in preparation for the School Leaving Certificate (SLC). From mid-1995, to complete Grades 11 to 12, I needed to study across the border in India.

At the beginning of each school session, the teachers would give us our timetable schedule. They didn't teach us in actual classrooms, it was more like a distance learning course. Every 15 – 20 days we would have to go back to the school to sit exams. We were given the topic of the exam during a tutorial and it was up to us to study and prepare for the exam. We were required to sit the exam within two days of the specified date. There was a library for us to use which was free but sometimes we would have to buy the books. I enjoyed studying and spent much time on my school work so that I was fully prepared when I went to the school and could ask my teachers any questions that needed clarification.

We were given assignments to take back to the camp but when we needed to sit for an exam we would catch several buses for the 3-4 hour journey to the school. I travelled with my friends and we kept each other company and shared a room between us to split the expenses. If the room was 500 rupees we would pay 250 rupees each. We also had to pay for the bus journey. I had a job working as a health worker in the camp assisting the medical doctors dispense medicine to the people. I saved the money that I earned and used it to study in India.

In 1996, whilst I was studying and working, I started spending time with a girl from my camp whom I really liked. We fell in love. It was a wonderful feeling. We spent one year getting to know each other. When we met, we would talk about how we could improve our lives and escape all the stress and hardship of the camp. She had a close relationship with her mother and being the oldest child they discussed all amongst themselves. After one year, I wanted to marry her. Her father was dead so I couldn't ask him for his daughter's hand in marriage. Her mother gave us her approval immediately. I felt extremely blessed because many young people have marriages arranged for them but I had fallen in love with my wife. No one chose her for me. We found each other on our own terms. It was such a special time for us.

We had our wedding in 1997 when I was around 20 years old and my wife joined us in our family hut which we shared with my parents. After three to four months, we were allowed to separate the hut into two sections so we could have some privacy. We didn't need our own hut, we just wanted a little privacy.

I began my university studies in that same year and continued to travel back and forth to India. During this time I learnt to speak Hindi.

My parents found it hard at the camp during this whole period as they had no money to spend and my father could not leave to work outside the camp. My parents were often upset and I would hear them talking about the property they owned and how good it was, compared to what they were struggling with now. Unfortunately, there were too many occasions where we didn't have enough food to eat and it was a depressing time for them experiencing the harsh changes that had been inflicted upon them.

Our first child Nissan was born in 1998 and he was such a cute baby boy. Initially, I only wanted one child so we used contraception which was available at our camp. After seven years, my wife wanted to have another baby and she said it would be so nice to have a little girl. Our beautiful daughter was born in 2006. We were both so happy to have a boy and a girl. I started teaching English at the camp school and that money was used to support our entire family.

In 2008, after living in the camp for over 18 years, the UN posted a sign and left leaflets at the postal centre where our letters would arrive. They explained the process and regulations for migrating to another country. I studied the leaflets and decided that it was necessary for us to change countries if our family was ever to have a better life. Many people were automatically sent to the USA with no choice but I was skeptical because of the news that we had heard about the World Trade Centre attack and other horrifying news about daily murders around the country. I was afraid to put my family in that environment. I started to research Canada and it seemed like the perfect country to fulfill our needs. I requested the change to the IOM (International Organization for Migration). Their office was located about 5-6kms away in Pedak and we needed to complete the process there. My wife and I rode my brother's bicycle to get to the office. I was the first in my family that decided to leave. After I completed the process, the rest of my family applied. Every night I would go to see the lady at the postal center, waiting anxiously for a letter.

Our letter finally arrived advising that we were accepted by Canada and that we would leave by the end of that year. The night before we left, all of my friends from school and my family came to join us for a big farewell party. I was 33 years old, my wife was 32, my son was 10 and my daughter was 2.

When we boarded the plane, we were nervous but excited at the same time. It was our first experience with flying. We had to catch two buses from eastern Nepal and then a plane to Kathmandu. We remained there for a few nights and then flew to Delhi and on to

Montreal via Zurich. It took nearly 24 hours from Kathmandu to Montreal and we were all extremely tired. We were part of a group of six families.

It was December 8th, 2008 when we arrived at Montreal airport. There was an interpreter waiting along with Line Chaloux, the amazing woman that pushed the door open for our migration to Canada.

It was -20 degrees Celsius when we arrived so they measured each of us for sizing and we were given coats, boots and head gear. A journalist spoke to us at the airport about our arrival and I was so tired, I barely knew what I was saying or didn't remember any of what I said when we left. When I finally saw the interview a few days later, we were all laughing at how my eyes were half closed and only then did I realize what I had said in the interview. They had a big bus for all 24 of us to travel in and when we arrived at the hotel, we were given cakes, fruit and other food but no one ate it as we were exhausted. We were at the hotel for eight days and Line came often to check that we had everything that we needed. My children were sick for three to four days because of the travel and sudden changes in food and environment. We gave them tablets to control the vomiting. My wife and I couldn't eat anything either. We had so much food provided but we couldn't tolerate the smell of food. We chose to drink water and juice. It took a while to adapt. On the 9th day we were given our apartment.

It was a nice change from the hotel room and we were taken to the local market where we chose our own food and vegetables like cauliflower, broccoli, lentils, rice etc. We ordered chicken because we couldn't find goat which was what we were used to back at the camp. It was such a blessing to have a home and prepare our own meals and those with which we were familiar. During that first week of settling in, people from the local Centre (the Coffret) came to see if we needed anything. My son started school within one week and they came to collect him and introduce him to the school.

The rest of us stayed in the apartment most of the time. It was snowing and we hadn't seen snow before. We would watch it every day on the mountains and initially we were fascinated by it. I decided to touch it so I took off my gloves and held it momentarily until I realized how very, very cold it was. After a few weeks, we were getting concerned about how cold it always was.

A French tutor came to help my son learn French and she taught us as well. Within two months, we started to learn the language and she assured us that the weather would get warmer by summer time. We didn't believe her until April came and it began getting warmer.

It took some time but we settled into our new life. We spoke with all of our family in Nepal and learned that my parents had different views about which country to go to. My father wanted to come to Canada and my mother wanted to go to the USA. It was decided that my father would come to Canada with one of my brothers and his family. My mother would go to the USA with my other brother, Narayan and both sisters. My father and brother arrived in Canada at the end of 2010 and it was wonderful to have some of my family around us. We often speak to the rest of the family in the USA and also to my brother Nerapati who is still in Nepal with his wife and children. He wanted to wait and hear about my experiences in Canada before deciding to join us.

We would love to visit Nepal one day when we can afford the trip, and maybe even Bhutan, but at this point in time, we are not allowed to return to Bhutan. It troubles me to remember or discuss how the police and army treated the Nepalese people in Bhutan. The government was to blame for that treatment. I believe there are still around 30,000 people in the camps but they are all slowly being sent to other countries for a better life.

It has been just over five years now. My family and I are almost fully integrated and are in the process of becoming Canadian citizens. Although the required paperwork is daunting, we are all so grateful to be here. My wife has started training to be an assistant chef and I have been utilized as an interpreter to practice all my skills and help others integrate. We have made wonderful friends here and once we adapted to the weather and learned French, life became even better. My children love playing in the snow and participating in all the winter activities here.

PART II

Refugee Stories II

Chapter VI

Refugee Story from Bhutan

My name is Bishnu and I was born in 1977 in a small country town in Salbandi Gou, Bhutan to parents of Hindu faith. When I was born my parents were overjoyed and relieved that they had created a new life because there were eleven children born prior to me and, sadly, four of them died tragically from a serious illness.

In order to provide for their large family, my parents needed to move to a warmer climate so that they could increase their income by growing more crops. Even though their three older daughters were already married and had decided to remain in northern Bhutan, they still had seven children to raise. I wasn't particularly close to my older sisters as they were so far away in the north of the country and I didn't get to know them very well.

Within one year of arriving in the south in 1971, four of their children, who were under five years of age, died and only three sons Puspalal, Yaduram and Gangaram survived. Losing four children in one year was indescribably painful for my parents. No one knows exactly the cause of their death but they believe it was related to the move the family made from the cool climate of northern Bhutan to the hot and humid sub-tropical climate of southern Bhutan. The four deceased children were buried near the house. A year later a little girl, Tulasha was born and I arrived six years later.

In Bhutan and Nepal, a family's and individual's social status is represented by one of approximately two hundred social classes. We are of the highest caste, the Brahmins. All Brahmin boys are eligible to become priests. My father taught my brothers about the Hindu religion and from the age of five, they were all sent to the local school to become priests. At school they also learned Nepalese and English.

The boys all studied for about ten years to become priests. Yaduram got married at the age of 13 and left for India to study at a higher level so that he could become a leader in his field. My father and brothers Puspalal and Gangaram are all classified as Brahmin Pupete and my brother, Yaduram is classified as Brahmin Panite, a slightly higher class. The different classes reflect the level of study achieved.

I stayed at home and helped my mother and sister with chores: I also helped on the land. When I was six years old, my mother gave birth to my sister Chandra Kala and five years after that to another girl Bima Devi. My mother kept falling pregnant because contraception was not commonplace.

My mother was a small woman who didn't say too much. She was, however, an extremely strong woman who ran the household and also helped out in the fields. She taught me to cook and I became the best cook in the family. I enjoyed this time with her. One of my favorite dishes contained rice, milk, sugar and cardamom – a very simple but tasty dish. The boys were studying and actively practicing Hinduism and, as it is against the religion to kill or eat animals, it was only the girls who ate fish and meat.

We were taught how to prepare all types of dishes. After preparing our meals, it was important to serve the food on separate dishes so that everybody could select what they could eat. Once the meal was finished, we cleaned all the dishes and would have to start cooking again to prepare for the next meal. As my brothers were away studying, we hired workers to come and help with the land and to also go fishing so that we had enough food for the large family.

Our family cultivated half our land and paid others to manage the other part. We sold all the produce from our land and just the nuts alone would make 45,000 rupees per year.

There were two houses on our land, we had many cows, sheep and goats and we would crop sugar cane, corn, beans, spinach, wool, and legumes. Each season required a new planting. We didn't need to buy from outside because the land provided us with everything we needed to eat. My sisters and I would milk the cows and we made butter with the cows' milk. We sold the butter and the milk to shops. At times we sold the animals too, but mostly just the cows. At times we sold small parcels of land to make money as it was a very big piece of land.

We were always busy either on the land or helping our mother. I remember my father and brothers would wake up at 4am every day and go to the temple that they had built inside our house to pray. They also studied in the temple during the day and later each evening, around 6-7pm, they would pray again. At times, my father invited other people to pray and chant with us.

My brother Puspalal got married and he and his wife had their first child at home with us. Yaduram was also married but was often away studying in India. The rest of us remained living together on our land.

In 1992, when I thirteen years old, my parents received a letter from a government agency informing them that the police were coming to the house on a stated date. I don't know what else was written in that letter but I could hear my parents talking in the other room and, when I looked in through the window, I could see them crying . My sister Tulasha had read the letter and said that it stated that the authorities would be coming to rape her and take my mother on a particular date. I don't have a copy of that letter because if you were found to have any official paperwork on you, you would be classified as 'a bad refugee', that is a lower class of refugee. Even the authorities in Nepal would imprison anyone who was found to be in custody of such papers.

Within two days of receiving that letter, we left behind the animals, our crops, our home and possessions and departed for India. My parents said very little to us. Their eyes were constantly filled with tears. They made this decision to avoid any of us being raped or killed.

We left at night so that we wouldn't be seen by the authorities. I remember that it was a very clear night with a full moon. It provided us with enough light to walk through the forest and across the border to India. We were following our parents and I was holding my sister Chandra Kala's hand. Tulasha was holding our youngest sister Bima Devi who was eight years at the time. My older brother Puspalal was leading his wife and young child. There were ten of us in all as Yaduram was still away studying in India. It took us half an hour to cross the border as we were not too far from it.

When we got to India, we went to stay with my father's friends. We stayed at their house for three weeks. My father tried to organize for us to stay in India but the Indian authorities were refusing to accept refugees from Bhutan. My father had no choice but to hire an auto bus to take us to Nepal. My brother Gangaram did not want to go to Nepal. His friends in Bhutan had told him that they too wanted to go to India but when he realized that he could not stay in India, he decided to return to Bhutan to be with his friends. When he arrived back at the border, he was told that he couldn't go back and he was arrested and thrown in prison. I kept asking my parents what was happening but they responded with "We are going to Nepal". I kept asking myself why we were going to Nepal. I thought we would return home in a few days.

The bus took seven hours to arrive in Nepal. After arriving at the camp, we all lived together in one hut for the first six months. It was an awful time for us as there was no water, no place to eat, a lot of sickness, often diarrhea because of the change in food. The camp was totally overcrowded and the authorities simply could not manage. There were many different religions in the camp: Buddhists, Hindus, Catholics and other Christians.
We lined up for water with our buckets and when the taps were

turned on, we needed to pump the water into the buckets. Although the United Nations gave us small amounts of food every week, many people were malnourished. I had never experienced such a lifestyle and it was a hard time for everyone.

We had made a lot of money from our farm produce in Bhutan and my father brought some of that money with us. After six months, he organized to buy us a better house and we were sent to a much smaller camp site with 2700 people and a much nicer house. In fact, we had two houses. My three sisters and I, along with our parents, shared the main house whilst my brother Puspalal shared a house with his family. My brother Yaduram came back from his studies in India to see his wife Harimaya who was living with her parents also in the camp. I was close to Harimaya.

The conditions were a lot nicer in this camp than what we experienced in the first camp. When Tulasha was 16, a man came to ask for her hand in marriage. My parents agreed and she left to live with her husband in his hut. All of us, except for little Bima Devi, got married in the camp and my parents chose our partners for life and where we would live.

My older sisters and their families from northern Bhutan joined us in Nepal and we all lived in separate camps, depending on where their husbands were placed.

When I was 18 years old my parents were friends with one of our neighbors whose nephew, Dhan Lal, often called to see him. My parents would visit them and I also got to talk with him. He was 22 years old and I liked him a lot. He lived at a nearby camp with his brother because his parents had remained in Bhutan. He was close to his uncle and one day, he came with his uncle and brother to ask for my hand in marriage. My parents agreed and one year later, we were married. Dhan Lal lived in another camp so I left to be with him in his hut. The camp I moved to had around 22,000 people in it so it was a big change for me.

The camp was set up like the other one in terms of the allocated lines A, B, C through to K. There was a shared toilet located between each two huts. Every day, each family was given their allocated letter which signified the time at which you could line up for water.

I began sewing traditional mens' hats and sold them to earn some money. We had our first child within 14 months and Dhan Lal and two of his friends took me to a hospital outside the camp on a stretcher. They took turns carrying the stretcher until we reached a truck that transported me to the hospital 30 minutes away. I was very tired from the drive to the hospital. I gave birth to my daughter in 1998 and I stayed in hospital for one day. When I got back to the camp my sister in law, Harimaya, stayed with me until all visits to meet the new baby in the family ended. Every month I went to my parents' camp and visited them with the baby. Meanwhile, I kept making the hats and selling them to the local mixed store that was set up in the camp.

My husband wanted to provide more for his family and new born child. As we needed things for our baby he left the camp and worked in Kathmandhu as a carpenter constructing houses. He would call us occasionally to tell us that he was alright and, when he could, he would send us money through other people. It was never very much money but it was something. He was away for two and a half years.

In 2000 my father died and I sent a message to Dhan Lal to come back. He was with us for only three weeks and then left again. The second time he was gone for three years. The next time he came back, he managed to stay for one year and it was then that I fell pregnant with my second daughter.

Dhan Lal left the camp in 2003 and vanished. No one knows what happened to him. I found it extremely hard to cope when he disappeared from our lives. I missed him a lot and I still do. My children never got to know their father and this has been a missing part of their lives. My neighbor at the camp kept an eye on the children for me if I needed to do something. I stayed at home looking after them and making hats until they were both at school.

In 2007 there was talk about a process that would enable us to change countries. My mother didn't want us to leave the camp but I needed to provide my children with a better life. We selected

Australia as our first option, and then Canada. We waited nearly six months to learn that we had been accepted by Canada. It was good news for me.

We had a farewell the night before we left and we stayed with my mother in her home. Everyone came to join us. We started our journey on 5th December 2008 and arrived in Montreal on 8th December.

Soon afterwards I phoned my family back in Nepal and told them that life was really good here. My daughters had been placed in school and I began to learn French. It was a big change for me to be on my own. I had left my entire family in the camp. My other sister also completed her process and left for the USA. My mother was really sad that her daughters were leaving her side. In May 2009, I spoke with her again on the phone and she told me that she had changed her mind and wanted to come to Canada to be with us.

In June, 2009 I spoke with Yaduram and he told me the sad news that our mother had fallen, hitting her head. She was sick for six days before she died. He and his wife were with her during this time. I kept thinking about the last time I saw my mother the night before we left Nepal. She was 70 years of age at the time. I remembered talking to her on the phone. She wasn't used to speaking on a phone so she kept it near to her ear and talked very loudly as she couldn't hear very well. She told me that she loved me and had started the process to be with us. That day never came and she was gone and I was so far away. I prayed a lot here in Canada when she died. I miss her. I have lost both my parents, my brother Gangaram is still in prison, and my husband has disappeared. It has been a tough and sad time for all the siblings.

In 2011 my brother Yaduram and his wife Harimaya came to Canada with their family. I was so happy to have them here. It has made such a big difference to me emotionally.

Three years earlier, before coming to Canada, my brother Yaduram was able to go and see Gangaram in prison as he had done once a year through the help of an organization in Nepal. Yaduram told us about the treatment that Gangaram was subjected to when he first arrived in prison. They used a torture machine on him which broke his arms and bruised his entire body as punishment for trying to re-enter Bhutan. Some time later, his legs were broken and he couldn't walk. These conditions continued until 2002. The same organization appealed to have punishment stopped. It was horrific to know what they did to him. My brother had devoted his entire life to being a priest and here he was being treated in this horrendous way in prison. He has now been there for 21 years. We have heard that he is still alive. On his last visit, Yaduram arranged to take my youngest sister Bima Devi with him. The conditions at the prison seemed to be a little better and Gangaram was happy to be able to see some of his family.

Gangaram is now 42 years old. Nobody can tell us why they won't release him. There are supposedly various political 'unexplained factors' involved. We really do not understand why something cannot be done. This is a beautiful man imprisoned for wanting to go home. It is not right.

My younger sisters Chandra Kala and Bima Devi are now in the USA and we speak often. My sisters from northern Bhutan have started the process to go to the USA. We have a big family in the USA. From what I know, there are approximately 60,000 Nepalese refugees that were sent to the USA and possibly 6,000 that have been sent to Canada.

In 2008 the people of Bhutan voted that it was the happiest country to live in. It has become one of the most expensive countries to visit and tourists/visitors are restricted to certain areas of the country. I do not know everything about Bhutan but I do know how our people were killed, raped and imprisoned. I am happy to be here in Canada and I look forward to becoming a citizen and being able to visit our family in the USA.

Chapter VII

Refugee Story from DRC

My name is Antoine and I was born in 1965. My parents had six children in the city and province of Kinshasa in the Democratic Republic of the Congo (DRC).

We were all born at the hospital of Kinshasa and raised at home by my parents. My oldest sister got married when I was five years old and she left to travel in Europe. I began school when I was six years old in 1971. I really liked school and made many friends. We spoke French at school and although the teachers also taught us English, I found it really difficult and tried to avoid it. Once my youngest brother started school, I looked after him to make sure he wasn't getting involved in any undesirable activities.

I got along well with both my parents and respected them for raising us well, paying for our school fees and giving us the opportunity to be educated. We were a middle class family. My mother took care of the house whilst my father worked in a government office. He had a car which allowed us to get about easily. After completing my homework, I helped my mother by doing my allocated chores such as sweeping the floors. If I needed any clothes or resources for school, my parents provided them for me. I was grateful to them for many things.

When I was about 10 or 11 years old, my father left for work one day and never came back home. We looked everywhere for him, in all the local establishments, the hospitals etc. My sister went to his work and asked them about him and no one knew anything. She eventually went to a detention camp near the home of President Mobutu and she found my father there. He was questioned by government officials at his office and detained because he was seen to be against President Mobutu. I was so upset that they had arrested him.

Six months later, I came home from school one day to find my father's broken wrist watch and glasses on the table. He had been released and it was good to have him back at home. I heard him talking with his friends and telling them how he was tortured and beaten by the guards. I know it was a hard time for him but he didn't tell me much about what he had gone through. I was too young to understand it all.

When I was 14 years old, my second sister got married and moved away to be with her husband.

In 1981, my father got terribly sick and kept telling me that he wasn't feeling well. I could see that he was suffering a lot. As we didn't know what was happening to him, we took him to the hospital but after three to four days, he died. They didn't do an autopsy on his body and his friends said that it was possible he had been given poison whilst in prison and that it took a few years to take full effect. Losing my father at the age of 16 was extremely difficult for me. His death had a devastating effect on the whole family.

I started dating girls in the local area. Two of the girls fell pregnant and both had a daughter. The little girls lived with their mothers. When I was 20 years old, my older brother got married and left home to start a life with his wife. I visited them over the years and enjoyed spending time with them.

I finished secondary school in 1988 when I was 24 years old but my grades weren't good enough to be accepted into university. I studied harder in order to go get a university placement.

In 1990 I was accepted into university and left my family home to study. I was 26 years old and it felt great being in the academic environment. I had news whilst I was away that my third sister got married and had moved away with her husband.

University opened many doors for me. At the time President Mobutu was in power in the DRC. I became a member of the Social Union for Democratic Politics which was a political party opposed to the President. We didn't like the way the government was running the country because any person deemed to be opposing the government was brutally arrested and, in many instances, killed. Many students wanted to take action and make a stand for democratic rights in their country.

Towards the end of 1991 I met a woman whom I wanted to marry and we made plans for a traditional wedding. Afterwards I continued my university studies whilst remaining totally involved in my political party.

President Mobutu organized a National Conference with a view to making some legislative changes and, at the same time, elect a new prime minister. We were in support of the conference but before it could take place, the reigning prime minister intervened and put a stop to the National Conference.

The students were very upset by this action and one of the Christian groups at the University organized a peaceful protest against the government.

The protest took place on 16th February, 1992. During the protest soldiers armed with weapons arrived in their trucks and surrounded our group so that nobody could leave. Two of the soldiers began striking me with their batons. They then took hold of one of my hands and dragged me along the ground for a long distance and threw me into the back of their truck with the other victims. My body had open wounds and I was badly bruised from the beating. The soldiers stood amongst the arrested students who didn't dare say a word.

They transported us to Makala prison where 15-20 of us were made to share one large cell. I was initially given some pain medication with minimal treatment for my wounds. It took me one month to recover from the beatings. We felt malnourished as we were only fed beans the entire time. At no time were we able to appeal against our imprisonment. We remained there until we were released six months later. I was forced to sign a paper stating that I would report every week to the prison officials and not go to any airport or border – this was so that I could not leave the country. I was forbidden to participate in any political events.

I went straight home and saw my wife and mother. They were relieved to see me safe and sound and they pleaded with me to refrain from participating in further demonstrations. I explained to my mother that I wanted to support the party that was trying to gain power and change our country's leaders. My father's death had a lot to do with my passion for driving political change in my country.

I was considered a student who was not afraid to be involved in any movement that could potentially bring change and others looked at me as a person of influence. I was a target for the police from my first arrest so I had to be careful with my involvement. Our liberty within our own country had been stripped away from us. I believed in taking a stance.

I began reporting to prison officials, however three weeks later I went to a meeting that was organized by my political party. It was held outside and our leader was giving a speech on a loudspeaker. It was a private meeting and I kept looking around for soldiers in case I needed to run, but there were none. A man came up to me stating that there was someone in a car that wanted to speak with me. I thought it was safe and that it was someone I knew. When I got there, I was pushed into the car and some men began beating me with batons as we drove away. They told me that I had been warned not to be involved in any political events. They beat me the entire time I was in the car and I was bruised and in pain from each blow.

They dragged me into an interrogation room, poured oil on the floor and placed an object at the other end of the room. They told me to lie down and swim to retrieve the object. I couldn't get to it because the oil did not allow me to grip the floor so I was swimming on the cement floor in the same position. They kept on beating me because I wasn't able to retrieve the object.

I was sent to prison to serve another six month sentence. Towards the end of my prison term in 1993 a prison guard approached me and told me to walk outside. He told me to get into a car and we drove off. I was forced to hide so that I wouldn't be recognized by anyone. As we drove away he told me that my uncle had organized for me to escape and that I couldn't be seen or else I would be shot on sight. I met my uncle at a friend's house. My wife and my mother arrived at the house shortly afterwards to see me. My wife was pregnant at the time. My uncle told me that I was to fly out of the country the following morning and I was to say goodbye to my family for the last time. I had not been married for long before I was imprisoned so my wife and I did not know each other in great depth and it was an awkward situation for us. My mother told me that she loved me and that had I listened to them and focused solely on my studies, I wouldn't be in this situation now.

The following morning my uncle gave me a travel document with my photo on it and I used that document to fly out of the country to Nigeria. I was alone when I flew out but my wife decided to follow me soon afterwards so that she could be with me when she gave birth to our child. We were living in a regular home in Nigeria when our first child arrived, a little baby girl.

I approached the United Nations, explaining my situation to them and was classified as a refugee in Nigeria. It was tough as a refugee as there were hardly any jobs and I had no money to support my wife and child. Within two years my wife fell pregnant again and the situation became worse. I was not used to living in such poverty and my wife was very unhappy. This affected our entire relationship. She decided to leave our daughter and me in Nigeria and she left, without a single word, fleeing to be with my mother in the DRC where she gave birth to our son.

Once our son was born she fled again, this time to Angola and she left our son in the care of my mother. I heard that she re-married and had more children with her next husband. We are not in contact.

My young daughter, who was living with me, was suffering because I did not have any money to support her and to be the father I needed to be. I spoke with my mother and made arrangements for my daughter to return to the DRC so that my mother could provide her with the care she needed.

I had four children by this stage, in different locations, and I was in constant communication with all of them. I kept following the news and keeping up to date with all the political changes in the DRC. I found minimal work as Nigeria has an extremely large population and employers do not want to give the few available jobs to refugees.

In 1999, I met a woman in Nigeria who was a refugee from the DRC. She fled the DRC because President Kabila had come into power and her parents and siblings were killed in their home. Luckily, she was away with one of her brothers at the time and the soldiers couldn't find them. A message was sent to her that her family were killed and she could not return home. As her great uncle was a general in the army at the time, she went to see him and he made arrangements for her to flee to Nigeria. He informed her that it was President Kabila who had ordered that her family be killed because her father refused to follow Kabila's orders. Her father was one of the soldiers in Rwanda that had helped bring Kabila to power. Many rebel groups had formed to fight against Kabila. Her father was ordered to fight the rebel groups but he refused. Due to his refusal Kabila sent soldiers to kill him and his entire family.

It was an extremely difficult time for her. We met under terrible circumstances but we understood each other and we fell in love and married in 2000. We lived as well as we could, trying to survive with what we had. We tried earning money in many ways, eventually buying and selling clothes. This seemed to work and provided us with some income.

My wife fell pregnant and gave birth to our son in 2003. The three of us were living together until my second eldest daughter from the Congo expressed her desire to join me in Nigeria. I made the necessary arrangements and she arrived in 2005.

Even though I kept going to the UN to explain our situation and to ask for financial assistance, the whole process was long and involved. Meanwhile, I had written an open letter and sent it to the Kabila government and a summary of that letter was published in the press.

I kept on telling the UN of the danger that I was in and after 2007, I was given an application form to apply for migration to another country. I was allocated Canada but we did not receive a confirmation of our acceptance until 2013.

We left for Canada in January, 2014 and for my son it was his first time on a plane. He started school immediately and, as he had only learnt English at school in Nigeria, he now needed to learn French here – I am sure he will learn quickly. My daughter is with us and, as she is much older, she is settling in well. My other two children will join us soon. My oldest daughter would also love to join us but as she is now 30, it is not so easy for her to come. Once you reach a certain age, you cannot be classified as a refugee with your parents. It is a separate application and a very expensive one.

We are grateful to be living in a country with such freedom. We were living a terrible life in Nigeria. We have been given a wonderful opportunity for a new beginning. I have been doing work in our house to make it even more comfortable for us. We have our basic needs here and, in time, I will be able to get my children a television so that we can watch it as a family group and a computer for my son to assist with his education. The people in this community have welcomed us warmly and we are very happy.

Chapter VIII

Refugee Story from the DRC

My name is Christian and I was born in August, 1960 in Kinshasa, the Democratic Republic of the Congo (DRC). I was the first of five children born to my parents. I was close to my entire family when we were together.

My father had three wives so I had three mothers at home who looked after the home and the children. My father was a successful businessman. He had ventures all around the DRC as he was in the construction industry, building homes and various other types of developments. He also owned stores that supplied construction materials, as well as restaurants and clothing shops. He worked hard, achieved a lot and I admired him for trying his best to get ahead in his business ventures.

He always told me to focus on my studies and to get a good education. Both my parents stressed how important it was to get married and have my own family one day.

At the age of 6 I started school at one of the best schools in the province of Kinshasa. I wore dark blue pants with a white shirt and, on special occasions, we wore a tie. I loved school. We were taught many subjects, including French and English, but I have forgotten the English since then.

In 1974, when I was 14 years old, I remember a teacher arriving from Belgium to teach at our school. His name was Montermans. He was the most inspiring teacher I'd ever had. He taught us mathematics and, by adding a little humor into his lessons, we would laugh a lot whilst learning a lot. It was a great way to learn. I made many friends over the years at school.

On occasions my father would take me on a business trip to some distant region to visit one of his stores. I didn't go all the time because I felt that I had to study. I was the oldest child and believed that I had a responsibility to set an example for my siblings by attending school and being conscientious. I enjoyed that responsibility and I believe that I was a good role model to them.

When I finished secondary school I studied engineering at university for one year but then decided to take a break and teach. I studied teaching but I didn't need an actual university degree to teach if I only taught junior students. I believed that if I gained experience working as a teacher this would help me in my university studies later on.

In 1986, when I was 26 years old, schools were on vacation break and I met a girl that lived in our local area but attended a school 300kms away. I fell in love with her but we couldn't see each other often because she was studying so far away. I continued teaching. I asked her to marry me and we decided to have a traditional marriage once she finished school.

We were married in 1991 in the DRC and it was a wonderful occasion. The marriage bonded our two families together. It is customary for the groom's parents to offer the bride's parents a 'Noix de Cola' or Cola nut, which is the caffeine-containing fruit of the Cola tree. We gave her father a pair of shoes and money and her mother some colorful material. We also provided a carton of quality cigarettes like Alaskan, Embassy Red or Green. Everyone had a great time and we were very happy. We didn't have our civil wedding to get our official papers until many years later in 2008 when we were in Chad.

Once we were married my wife came to live with us in our family home in the capital, Kinshasa. We were ready to start a family immediately and by the following year in 1992, we had our first child, a beautiful baby boy. I promised my wife that if our first child was a boy, I would get her a wonderful, extravagant gift like a car but I haven't fulfilled that promise yet because I didn't have the means to do that on a teaching salary. After my son was born, there were many teachers' strikes occurring so I stopped teaching for a while and began working as a guide on river boats transporting people. I also sold all kinds of small articles to get by.

Our second child, a son, was born three years later in 1995. It was a wonderful feeling to have two healthy children. My wife spent her days keeping house and looking after the children and as I needed to earn more, I resumed teaching.

In 1997 war erupted in the east of the country. Rwandan soldiers and Congolese rebels were financed by the Rwandan and Ugandan governments to invade the DRC. They were making their way to Kinshasa.

On 17th May that year, I awoke and went to work as usual. I was watching the children play football on the field when I suddenly saw people running frantically in every direction. They shouted out that the rebel groups had infiltrated the whole city. The war had started and the whole town was in fear. I raced home to my family and told my wife that we needed to leave immediately with the children. Three of my sisters were home at the time but my parents and other sister were nowhere to be found.

Kinshasa is close to another capital city, Brazzaville of the Republic of the Congo. These are two of the closest capitals in the world at just 1.6 kms apart. We decided to cross the river and go to Brazzaville. Local fisherman helped my family cross the enormous river in a small African paddleboat. There were people running everywhere, some also trying to cross the river. Many people were scared to cross the river. My sisters decided to go further inland instead of crossing the river at this point. That was the last time I saw my sisters.

When we got to the other side, we were kept in groups at the docks for two days whilst people still desperately tried to cross the river. I saw my neighbor cross over and he told me that he had seen my other sister, that she was okay but that my father had been shot dead by one of the rebels as he was running away. It was one of the worst experiences of my life to hear that my father had been killed in that way. I was overcome with sadness and panic and cried uncontrollably for a very long time.

The police at the docks helped us find some sheets and some food for my children. We had to think of something to do. We had nothing and we couldn't live like this. We began hiding with the other families in little hangars in the docks where they stored the boats. We stayed there for two weeks. We knew that we had to leave but we had no money to travel. I had to find a way of getting us out of there. It was the first time in my life that I asked for charity. It was so difficult and I was not proud of our situation at the time. I had no other choice if my family was to survive. They needed to eat. Some local people gave us a little money, some clothes and food. With that money we paid a boat owner to take us a long way up the river to the Central African Republic. We settled in the capital, Bangui where there was a community of citizens from the DRC. We met with the leader of the group and he offered us shelter in his home for a few days.

It was a small home and it was not big enough for all of us. In that part of the country, you could rent an apartment and pay the rent at the end of the first month, rather than upfront. We rented a home and I tried to find any job just so that we could survive. We realized quickly that the town people didn't like outsiders. There was xenophobia and racism and minimal hospitality was extended to us. I worked as a teacher but often they didn't pay me. There was also a high risk of me being attacked or killed when coming home at night. It was an extremely insecure time. I couldn't contact my family as I didn't know where any of them were.

After seven months we decided to leave Bangui. We had heard that Chad was far more hospitable and we arrived there in 1998. I went to the United Nations office and explained our situation. They accepted our paperwork and by 1999 we were given refugee status. The UN High Commission for Refugees was still in development at the time in Chad so it was the United Nations that gave us our cards.

Once the office of the UN High Commission for Refugees was opened they organized an interview for us and it went really well. The process for us to be on a list for assistance had begun and we were very hopeful. In 1999 we had our third child, a baby girl, and in 2002, we had our fourth and last child, also a little baby girl. I was proud of our family and I love them dearly.

I started teaching and also tutored children in their homes. It paid for our rent and food and enabled us to survive. We didn't live in a refugee camp and were able to stay in the city as urban refugees. My wife had been sewing clothes for many years and she could help out by earning an income when we needed it. It also gave her an interest whilst looking after the children.

In 2004 I decided to go back to University in Chad and study French Literature and French Linguistics. The UN High Commission of Refugees (UNHCR) paid my tuition fees. My children were going to school and I helped them with their studies wherever possible.

My wife began to have serious medical problems from 2006 onwards. We saw many doctors but they couldn't help. We travelled to the hospital in Cameroon but they couldn't cure her. They tried different methods but they were unsuccessful. The UNHCR sent us to see a specialist in Chad and he told us that she couldn't be treated in Africa as they didn't have the resources to perform the surgery. The problem was in her abdominal area, a delicate part of her body, and it caused her constant pain. I told the UNHCR the outcome from the specialist appointment to see if we could find another solution.

On 2nd February 2008 war broke out on the streets around us and there was a huge crossfire between the government soldiers and the rebel groups from Sudan. The rebels were coming in trying to take power. So many of these wars throughout Africa are based on power and leadership. We were caught between the two parties and people were running everywhere to escape the conflict. Both groups kept fighting and people were being killed all around us. We were stranded for two hours hiding in a shelter whilst the shooting and bombing continued around us. We had to run from the shelter to another district to find somewhere safe to survive. The children were running beside us and, as the little ones were still very young, we kept on telling them to keep running as fast as they could. They ran so well, even when they had to climb over piles of dead bodies. I can only imagine what they were feeling at such a young age to be exposed to such traumatic experiences and frightening sights. The youngest was six years old at the time and our eldest was sixteen.

We saw a place that looked like an office building and it was right in front of the military base camp where the Government Palace was located. There were army tanks everywhere. The whole sector was covered with rebels who were going from house to house, killing anyone in their way and making their way towards the palace. The President had given orders to the Chad army to bomb everywhere near the Palace to try and scare off the rebels, even if there were local citizens hiding in the houses.

I will never forget the sound of the bombs numbing our ears. All around us were the uninterrupted blasts of heavy weapons and gun fire. There was no silence for a second. As we entered the building, there were other families already hiding in there and they tried to help us hide. They told us that we were 300 meters from the French army base. The French had positioned themselves in certain points in the city with heavily armed weapons to protect the schools and institutions in the area.

We were extremely blessed on this day and some miraculous angels must have watched closely over our family.

Momentarily, at 10.30 that morning, there was a break in the crossfire whilst negotiations between the leaders took place. During this period of ceasefire, the French army courageously went from house to house trying to find refugees and save civilians.

French soldiers found us and, after seeing our papers, told us that they would take us to their base for protection. The negotiations failed and the fighting resumed but we were in the safest possible place at the time.

At the base we met a family from Rwanda who explained the situation at the French Army camp. We were provided with food, medical assistance and anything else we needed. We slept there that night in army beds and we could hear the bombs blasting throughout the night.

The following morning at 11am we were put on a huge cargo plane. We entered through the back hatch and we sat on the sides where the soldiers normally sit because the plane shakes and vibrates a lot and the sides are the safest place to sit. The seats are removable so that tanks and equipment can be loaded. We had to hang on to our seats because of all the shaking.

We were flown to an army base in Gabon where we were well looked after by the French Army and the Red Cross. My wife was still battling with her sickness and at times she couldn't breathe. They tried to help her by giving her medicine but she was still very unwell. We stayed in Gabon for 21 days until the war stopped. The government of Chad was victorious against the rebels and we were taken back to Chad. The government organized for all the bodies to be collected and cleaned up the entire area.

Our home was damaged. The door was broken, some items were damaged and others stolen as street bandits had come through and looted the houses.

Our life went back to normal fairly quickly and there was tranquility again. We never returned to the area where we hid that night as we found it too traumatic. I kept visiting the UN High Commission as often as I could to check on our status because the trauma of the war and my wife's illness made it an extremely difficult and emotional time for us as a family. I continued to study for my degree and in 2012 I completed my studies.

In 2013 we were informed that the High Commission had organized for us to go to Quebec, Canada. We are so grateful to the U.N. High Commission and the Canadian and Quebec governments for giving us relief from our hardships and offering my family a chance of a happy and safe future.

When we arrived we were set up in an apartment and provided with all our basic needs. My children were able to go to school immediately and even though the French is different and all systems are completely unfamiliar to us, we are all adapting well. My wife is completing her secondary school studies in Mathematics, French and other subjects and enjoying the experience of studying with other people. She had surgery in February 2014 to help improve her medical condition and she seems to be improving day by day. I know we are the lucky ones to have found freedom at last. Being of

Catholic faith, we believe that we were blessed the entire time.

The weather here in the colder months is hard to adjust to. Some refugee and immigrant children told our kids that their noses would fall off and their ears would snap if they stood in the cold for more than thirty minutes. For a while they were afraid that that would happen.

I need to find a job and, if the government recognizes my studies, I will be able to go to work soon and earn a better income for my family. My wife has decided to study nursing once she has recovered so that she can help others. My children need computers for their studies and we will need a family car, especially in the cold winters. We have to catch taxis to get our groceries and it is expensive to do that regularly.

I was able to get in touch with one of my sisters recently. She told me that my mother (pictured below) had died from a heart condition in the DRC but no one knows exactly when. It is so upsetting to remember what happened to my parents during the war and to wonder what happened to my other sisters.

My mother

My wife's family also fled from the war at the same time as mine. My wife was able to recently get in touch with her mum and to find out that they are now safely back in Kinshasa. It is so sad to have a first-hand experience of war and to know that millions of innocent people are slaughtered by rebels or killed in the crossfire of these conflicts every day in certain countries in the world.

We are grateful for our freedom and glad that we had faith and belief along the way that one day we would have a new life in a country without war. I am now 54 years old and believe that my family have a wonderful future, full of opportunities, ahead of them.

Chapter IX

Refugee Story from Bhutan

My name is Rupa and I was born in 1987 in Bhutan. At the time of my birth, I had two older brothers, Bikash and Rupesh. Together with my parents we lived in our own home in a village in rural Bhutan.

I don't remember much about living in Bhutan and most of my memories are molded from my parents' description of their former life. My parents worked transporting fruit and produce to other villages in the area.

With the deteriorating situation in Bhutan for people of our ethnicity, my parents were forced to do many things with which they struggled. The authorities would make them ask others for money and force them to go to other peoples' farms and forcibly take animals, such as chickens, from their homes. I know they did not want to do those things but they were given an ultimatum that they either bring them what they demanded or they would come and rape the women in our village, including my mother. My parents were extremely traumatized and put under extreme pressure.

As a direct result of the king's orders, the government authorities took away our cultural liberty, values and traditions. During that period my parents were forced to speak Dzongkha which is the national language of Bhutan. No one was allowed to speak our native Nepalese language and everyone was forced to wear the local clothes of the ethnic majority. It was terrible because the price people paid when they didn't obey was a price that no one should ever have to confront: you were killed and, if you managed to avoid death, prison was the alternative.

In 1991 when I was four years old, conditions were out of control for the Nepali minority who called Bhutan home. My parents had no desire to speak Dzongkha or wear the clothes they were forced to wear, nor to live each day with the fear of getting killed or raped.

My mother had just given birth to my little sister and she was nine days old when our lives changed. As night set in, with a new born baby in my mother's arms, we left our home and everything in it to walk across the border to Nepal. I remember the darkness, the pitch black darkness.

When we reached the camp in Nepal, there were many other people from Bhutan already there. We were assigned to the Khudanabari camp and we began life in section B3, hut 99. As I was still very young when we got there, I don't remember what effect all this change had on my parents. My older brothers and I went to school in the camp. When I was eight years old, my mother gave birth to my baby brother. Before and after school I would help my mother take care of my little brother and sister.

I had a good relationship with my mother. In our culture, we must respect our parents and always listen to them, even beyond 18 years of age. I always obeyed my mother. My relationship with my father was also good, however he often went outside the camp for work so he wasn't at home much. At times, if the weather was good and there was no rain, he would leave for two to three months at a time.

My older brothers and I continued to go to school until Bikash and Rupesh were old enough to go and work with my father outside the camp.

I noticed that many people drank alcohol in the camp. It made them relax. Both my parents drank. I am not sure what type of alcohol it was, although it looked clear like water. My mother battled with serious medical issues having low sugar levels and high blood pressure. The more she drank, the more at risk she placed her health.

By the time I was 13 years old in 2001, my mother's blood sugar levels were so low one day that she suddenly fell down and died. I always remember her as a strong, tall woman but with all the drinking and her deteriorating condition, there was no more hope of recovery or survival. She was Hindu but we could not have a traditional burial for her. It was a hard time for all of us as my little sister was eight and my youngest brother was only five. I became their mother figure.

My father was 43 years old at that time and now under even more pressure to work harder to provide for us. My brothers kept going with him outside the camp to work and make money. I would stay and look after my younger siblings.

When my father returned from work, he would stay two or three weeks at a time. Occasionally he was there for one or two months so when my siblings and I came home from school, he would have dinner prepared for us. He would speak about my mother often, crying when he spoke of her. I could see he missed her. He was never interested in marrying again. People in our culture believe that when a man marries again it is never good for the children as the stepmother doesn't care for the children as she does for her own. Their belief is that it becomes too hard for the children so my father stayed alone.

At times he would go outside the camp to a nearby village to work during the day so he could be back home at night with us but that was only for a short time. He was drinking heavily when he was home and it got to the point where he was spending all the money on alcohol and not taking care of us.

Meanwhile, my older brother Bikash fell in love and married an Indian girl which meant that he spent his time with her.

My sister and I were battling with our own illnesses and after my mother passed away, my father converted us from Hinduism back to his Christian faith. We started to go to the local Pentecostal church that was set up in the camp where the pastors would help us pray and talk to us positively about our situation. We developed an extremely strong faith and it was this faith that made us feel better every time we were unwell. The pastors would explain to us about life and that death is a part of life. They helped us with food and we were extremely grateful that we had them at the camp.

We would tell them about our father's drinking and how he wasn't able to take care of us because he was spending all the money on alcohol. It made it hard for us to care for him when he was always drunk. I know that he was depressed for many years since my mother's death and the stress of the whole situation would have been extremely difficult for him to handle. The alcohol helped him to relax. The only time he would not drink was when we went to church to see the pastors. Even the pastors tried to talk with him and explain that life was like that and now he needed to be strong to look after his children. Nothing they said seemed to work. He continued drinking and often when he came across the pastors in passing, he would run the other way to avoid them.

I was in charge of the household and had to continue looking after my brother and sister. When my father and brother were away, which was most of the time, I was able to get their allocation of a 5kg bag of rice every 15 days. Everyone in the camp was allowed one bag. I would take their bags and sell them to other people in exchange for money. I used that money to buy vegetables for us.

In early 2008, after 18 years at the refugee camp, we started the paperwork process to come to Canada. Sadly, in mid-2008, my father's drinking got worse and he was taken to the local camp hospital. They told us that he had a heart problem and sent him to a hospital outside the camp. Within three days, he died. His body was sent back to the camp from the hospital and we buried him at the camp.

We were orphans at this stage and we knew we needed a better life. My older brother Bikash didn't complete any paperwork because he wanted to stay with his Indian wife. My brother Rupesh had met a Nepalese girl who was being sent to the USA so he went with her to the USA. I was the only one left and, at 20 years of age, was caring for my sister who was 15 and my baby brother who was only 12. Due to our situation of having no parents, our paperwork was expedited and we ended up being one of the first families to leave the country for Canada.

I didn't know what lay ahead for us so I was anxious about the whole issue. A few people at the camp told us scary stories about being in Canada. They told us to make sure we lock the doors as black men with piercings would appear at your door and come in to hurt you. I didn't like hearing stories like that as it scared us all. We really had no idea what to expect and without parents, we all had to be brave. We had nothing and no money to support ourselves but we had faith that all would be okay.

There was only a total six families from the seven different camps departing for Canada and we were the only family to leave from Khudanabari. They had a bus waiting for us to take us to the airport. My brother made a friend very quickly to keep him company on the plane and they sat a few seats behind us. I thought he was scared but when I looked behind, they were both looking out the window feeling excited by this new experience of flying in the sky.

The flight was so long for us and by the time we got to Montreal we were extremely tired. All the families were in the same state. As we walked inside the terminal, my brother was on my left and he started to vomit. By the time I tried to help him and clean up the vomit, my sister started to vomit. The long flight, the change in food and the lack of sleep affected us all.

During our first week, immigration officials collected us to have our photos taken for identification purposes and took us to the bank to set up an account. We were assisted with everything else that we needed to do. Back at the camp, I was taught basic English at school, but not French. We realized fairly quickly that everyone spoke French in the province of Quebec and that we would need to learn French.

After the first week we were introduced to a beautiful retired couple who volunteered to look after us. They used to be doctors and they helped us with so many things. We call them mother and papa. The moment the immigration officials found a government apartment for us, they came and helped us settle in the apartment. We felt safe and cared for by them. They showed me how to get the mail and explained what paperwork we needed to complete. They helped us set the phone service up so that we could call my brother in Nepal. They were a real blessing.

Once the three of us were alone in the apartment we couldn't believe how big it was. It had two rooms for us to share but we were so scared, having heard the terror stories from the camp, that for the first two months we all slept together in the same room, in the same bed.

One day soon afterwards the immigration people came to take me to Winners Clothing Store to get some clothing for my siblings and me. I was busy shopping when mother and papa arrived with my little sister who was crying hysterically. They told me that after I left with the officials, they were waiting at home and someone knocked at the door. When they opened the door, an African delivery man with a piercing had come to deliver a table. When my sister saw him, she immediately panicked thinking he was going to attack her, remembering the story that we had been told at the camp. My brother wasn't afraid but as my sister was terrified and started squealing, my mother and papa had to bring her to me. She was 15 years old.

After two months of settling in, my brother started using the other bedroom. We were informed that being twelve years old he would start at the local secondary school. On the morning of his first day at school, my sister and I put on our coats and boots and walked him to the traffic lights. We explained to him that if he didn't cross in time, a car would hit him so he would have to walk immediately when the walking light flashed. He turned to me and said, "Okay sister, sit nicely". As soon as we saw the flash, we yelled, "go brother, go". We waited until he was safely across the road. We both then began to cry because our brother was leaving us to go to school and with tears in our eyes we walked back to the apartment. We were waiting for him at 4pm when he was on his way home.

It was important for us to be within walking distance of everything we needed. We didn't have money to buy a car and it was important for us to be near a church. Our mother and papa are both Catholic and we went with them to church every Sunday. We had the option of living closer to the other Nepalese families in order to make our migration easier. However, for us, our faith in God was a priority and we wanted the sanctuary of a church nearby.

In 2009, after settling in for nine months, I began taking French lessons. It was also then that I started getting very sick. I would vomit frequently, have extremely painful migraines and my entire face and my feet would swell. I felt tired and my blood pressure was very high. One Saturday evening we were invited to dinner with another Nepalese family and soon after we arrived my headache intensified and I was in excruciating pain. Mother and papa took my blood pressure. It was an extremely high reading. When I arrived home I began vomiting. I tried to sleep but by Sunday morning, I was still vomiting. My brother called our mother and she told him that he needed to get me to a hospital. After doing many tests, the hospital staff explained that my kidneys were damaged so severely that they had stopped working. They sent me to another hospital in Montreal where I stayed for one month. I cried all the time because my little brother and sister were home alone without me. I was their mother figure now and they relied on me. I had to stay in the hospital for dialysis. After one month, they finally let me leave but every Monday, Wednesday and Friday I still go to the hospital for dialysis. The hospital gave me a pager and told me that I was on the list to get a kidney transplant but they were not sure how long it would take. As I couldn't go to French lessons and had to stay at home, I was extremely bored. People told me that I was sick and that I wouldn't be able to do anything because of my kidneys. I don't like to think that way. We have come from a country where we worked hard to survive. We had no cars, no resources to make life easier; we carried heavy items on our heads and walked for long distances to go anywhere. I don't consider the type of work I have seen here to be as difficult as to what I did back home. I wanted to push myself here and move forward towards my future.

We have been here for six years now. My sister fell in love and married a Nepalese boy and is now living with his family here in Canada. My older brother Rupesh married his Nepalese girlfriend in the USA and now has his home there. We talk with my brother Bikash in Nepal whenever we can. Only my younger brother and I now remain at home. He is 18 years old and still goes to school. Through the help of our mother and papa, my brother was able to get a part-time job at a local restaurant and he loves his work. We don't have much money to live extravagantly, we just get by with what we have but we are happy and grateful for all that life has given us.

I have been going to the local center (the Coffret) to participate in the 6 month 'integration into work' program scheme five days a week from 9-4pm. Not having a car makes it hard in the cold weather to get to the hospital for my dialysis, but I manage. I still go to the hospital three nights a week for four hours at a time for my treatment. I am often exhausted but I am happy. I have made friends and I can now read so life is a lot better.

I think about my parents and how they died and I miss them. I see how children speak to their parents here at times and I think to myself that if I had loving parents like that, I would treat them with reverence and never in such a disrespectful manner.

I am happy in Canada. This is our home now. Maybe one day, when we can afford it, we may visit Nepal and Bhutan, but for now we are settled. I would love a donor to come forward and offer me a kidney and I remain hopeful that that will happen. In the meantime, I am grateful for the love and support of our mother and papa here in Canada and I want them to know just how much they mean to all of us. We love them very much.

Chapter X

Refugee Story from Mauritania

My name is Aiden and I was born in 1958 in Kaedi, Mauritania in Africa. Kaedi is located in the very south of the country, close to the border with Senegal. I was raised in the Muslim faith and studied the Koran. I have raised my children in the same faith and also teach them the Koran. I believe in God, that he created us all and I believe in Jesus and all the prophets. There are 24,000 prophets that I acknowledge and about twenty five prophets that I follow closely – my main prophet is Muhammad. I grew up in a household where we prayed five times a day. No matter what we were doing at the time, we had to stop and focus on our prayers. We cover our entire bodies when we pray. Our women are not required to wear a burka and wear long dresses and turban-like headwear, leaving their faces exposed.

Within our faith, it is legal for us to have up to four wives and it is against our religion to have mistresses. My father had several wives so I always had many mothers around me. Each of them generally treated all the children as their own and shared the responsibility of raising another wife's children. All children call each mother by her first name. It is a very different household concept to many other parts of the world.

Home births are very normal in Mauritania and that is why so many people don't have identity papers. Often, in later life, the age of a person has to be estimated and that can lead to a difference of many years. I am 62 years old now but on my documentation, I am 57. It is so difficult to accurately monitor age details when many children are born by different wives. Many African births are allocated 1st January if an exact date is not known.

I have two older and one younger brother. My parents are both still alive and living in Senegal. My father is 98 years old and my mother is 79. They are both mentally alert and coherent, aware of everything that is going on and I speak to them often. In Africa, parents are allowed to hit their children for disciplinary reasons but my parents never enforced that upon me. I only ever saw that when one of the children did something extremely bad.

I completed my primary schooling in Africa and when I was eighteen years old, I started working as a mechanic for a big company. As other employees, every year I would sit an exam, do an internship in the next level and progress to the next level within the company. The company was located in the mine region and we serviced and repaired mine company vehicles. I worked on buses, taxies, cars, and motorcycles etc. We fixed everything that needed to be repaired. I worked for this company for around twenty years and was the manager of my team.

During this time, I lived in a compound that was compromised of several houses. I married four women over the years and had children with each of them. I would sleep for two nights with each wife in their separate rooms. One of my wives was blind but she looked after the children and cooked as well as the other wives. She had been blind since the age of five and her condition could not be cured. She did everything and you couldn't tell that she was blind by looking at her. She was very experienced and highly independent when taking care of the house. However, we always ensured that one of the children was with her when I couldn't be there.

In 1989 war broke out in our town. It was an uprising against black people by the 'Moors'. It was an ethnic war based on racial issues and the conflict quickly spread throughout the entire population. The director of our company was a white French man who cared about all his workers.

One day during the war, whilst at work, my director explained to us that the 'Moor' government was trying to locate black people on their list. When found, these people would be beaten and tortured. We were right in the middle of the war zone and it was a tough time for everyone; we all lived in fear. I had already been tortured during this time and have terrible memories of this whole period. The director organized for the United Nation (UN) military guards to come in and protect his black workers by taking us to another location. He was very kind to us.

The guards came in trucks and they transported us to an island as a temporary measure. When I arrived, there were already many black people on the island. The UN arranged for France and Morocco to send planes and remove us from the war zone. We were flown to Senegal and placed in a refugee camp.

A few weeks later my parents, wives and children took a boat along the river from Mauritania to Senegal. From there, a truck transported them to the camp in Senegal.

Living as a refugee was tough. We began in the refugee camps and I had to support the entire family. Every morning I walked for many kilometers to go and register my name with the United Nations. They gave me a little money and I would use that money to go into the city and buy groceries for the family. I had three wives at the time and a separate room with each.

My wives kept having children so I registered to work with individuals who worked in construction. They wouldn't give the refugees the big jobs so I would work mixing cement or unloading trucks to earn $2 - $4 per day. I rarely slept as I had to work as much as I could.

Although my older daughters got married and went to live with their husbands, with all the younger children in the family, it was difficult for everyone. I eventually decided to keep only one wife, the one that was blind, and ended up divorcing my three other wives.

I met a man who owned many houses and managed to find us another place to live. It had only one room but it was close to the city and we stayed there whilst I tried to find work. There was a little garden with some animals and the boys helped maintain them while I was away at work. We stayed in Senegal until 2008.

I applied to the United Nations requesting that my family and be sent to another country. We had no money for the children to go to school and no money for medical needs. I lost five children that were sick because I couldn't afford healthcare – they died in our arms. It was such a traumatic period in our lives. The paperwork to leave the country took so long to be cleared because I had so many children with different wives. Not all the children had paperwork and some of their birth dates had to be estimated. I applied to take all the children that were living with us at the time to another country. There were ten children ranging in ages from four to seventeen years of age.

My wife and I came to Canada with all ten children. It was tough on the older ones because they hadn't had a true education; I had only taught them the Koran at home. I also continued to teach them to respect their elders as I believe that people must always assist the elderly when they can. If the children do anything wrong, they get grounded and with so many of them running around the house, it is always full of commotion and hard to manage. My wife is a very strong woman to cope with overseeing ten children whilst being blind. She was pregnant when we first arrived but the baby died two weeks before she was due and she is buried here in Canada.

I talk to the rest of my daughters in Africa and maybe one day they can come here too. One of them goes to school and I send her money to pay for her education. We have settled here well and when I can get a secure job, I will be able to provide my children with more of their needs. We have our basic necessities and we get by.

I am 63 years old now, but on paper, I am 58 years old. My children have a much better future here than what they would have had in Africa and that was my main motivation for moving away from our birth country. I need to concentrate on feeding my family and paying our bills as there are a lot of mouths to feed in my family. I spend my time focusing on what lies ahead and rarely think about our past which has left a deep and heavy scar in my heart.

One of my sons would also like to share a little of his past and his aspirations for the future.

My name is Bomani and I am nineteen years old. I didn't go to school in Africa as I had to help my brothers in the garden. There were many gardens we worked in, one of which belonged to my uncle. I helped with all of them. I awoke early and sowed the seeds. I also helped my older brothers to take care of our animals. When I was around twelve years old, my father gave me Koran lessons.

I had many friends in Africa from the local area and I miss them very much. I think of them often, especially during festivals, such as Eid at the end of Ramadan. I would like to be with them because I know we would have a lot of fun.

Soon after we received confirmation regarding our move to Canada, I saw a TV program about Canada and it was snowing. I found that interesting at the time but when we got here I realized just how cold it can get. That was something that I could never have imagined beforehand.

I remember being on the plane to Canada; initially I was scared because we were all seated separately but then it became such an exciting experience. School was a totally new and different experience for me as I had never been before. I made friends easily and although we played sport together, I couldn't speak with them because I didn't speak French. There was one lady at school who could understand my native language, Peul, but apart from her, no-one understood me. It was hard to adjust at first but it is a lot better now that I have adapted to school and am learning French.

I love music and I love writing lyrics and singing songs. I would love to be an actor one day as I love participating in the film camps.

As my brother now lives on his own, I live in a house with eight other children – but I don't mind them. They don't bother me. I have my own room and I get by. We don't have much money but it's okay. I remember back in Africa, my friends and I used to poke fun at my younger sisters and try to ruin their games and annoy them. I am older now so I don't do that here but I still laugh at those memories.

I would love to go back and visit one day. We were raised with many mothers and I hope that one day I can go back and see my birth mother. I would love to send her money but I need to get a job here and finish my schooling first. I am registered as being fifteen years old on my official papers, and as frustrating as this can be, it's a common refugee problem. Birth dates of so many children can be confused during war times. On a positive note, this complication has allowed me to complete my secondary school studies.

Having been raised in Africa and seeing the way we live here now, I would like to send a message to others. We are all equal. Just because I am black and I come from Africa, people shouldn't judge me. I have been faced with some racial abuse but I ignore it. I like to write positive messages about the need to eradicate ignorance, insults and judgment. Without these negative traits, we can all live happier lives. I am hoping to convey these messages through my songs of romance, love and hope.

PART III

LINE CHALOUX

The following is the life story of Line Chaloux.

This personal account demonstrates that even though many of us are born into a loving, peaceful and sometimes privileged environment, without ever being exposed to any of the traumas and tragic circumstances of the refugee community, we can open our minds and hearts and become determined to help others less fortunate than us.

As you learn about Line's family history, you will appreciate how her ancestors and loved ones played a vital role in her life and laid some foundations for her to become the humanitarian and amazing individual that she is today. You will also discover her continued efforts to succeed and overcome challenges.

Line is a true inspiration.

Chapter XI

Line Chaloux; Part One

My story starts before I was born. I am sitting on a mountain, a gigantic mountain, and beneath me is a valley surrounded by more mountains. In fact, there is a place in Saint Adele, in Quebec, Canada that looks exactly like this place. I am on the mountain with many other people. It's as if we are having a big picnic and we are surrounded by a warm light that fills us with love. I feel this love through the light until suddenly I hear "Okay, you can go". At that exact moment I was born. It was 10th February, 1958 and it's as if I chose to be born at that precise time when I knew that I had something significant to accomplish.

In the 1700's two brothers with the surname Chaloux sailed from France to Quebec, Canada. Our entire Chaloux family are descendants of these two men. We are a big family and most of us live in Saint Jerome, Quebec.

The first brother married a First Nations Native American woman from the Clan of the Turtle. They settled in the Laurentians region of Quebec and remained there for many generations. My maternal great grandmother Clara Bourgeois and her family were among the first to settle in this area. She was baptized by Father Labelle, the priest credited with the colonization of a major part of Quebec.

Prior to my birth, my parents had three other children, all boys. The eldest was called Michel and we became very close later in life. The second son, Alain died at three months of age, and the third son died at birth. At the time, as there were no funeral homes and, as was custom, Alain was displayed in the living room for three days, after which he was buried. When the third-born son died my mother could not cope with having her departed child lying in rest in the living room. The doctors gave my father his deceased baby in a box and the burial took place immediately. It was extremely difficult for my parents to experience the devastating loss of two children in close succession.

Shortly after the death of her two sons, my mother's father, Paul-Emile Lamoureux also passed away so I never knew my maternal grandfather. After these family deaths, my birth was considered a true blessing. I was not allowed to die. I was considered a precious gift and everyone showered me with an abundance of love and care, especially my parents and my maternal grandmother, Jeanne Daoust.

I was extremely close to my grandmother Jeanne as she was always at home and looked after me much of the time. She made sure that I was never cold or hungry and that I never needed to ask for anything as it was already provided. From a very young age there were a lot of good and caring people around me and I developed great confidence because of the love that was bestowed on me. I considered myself to be a very lucky young girl as I was aware that it wasn't the same for everyone in this world.

My grandmother Jeanne and I

By the time I was old enough to understand the deaths of my two older brothers, I believed that my soul had already tried unsuccessfully on two previous occasions to come into the world as a male and only succeeded the third time as a female. It made no difference to me whether I was a boy or a girl.

I was a small baby and my brother Pierre, born two years later in 1960, was quite tall. At a young age we looked like twins. My parents used to dress us in similar outfits. I would wear a shirt and red skirt whilst he would wear a shirt with red pants.

My sister, Marie Josée was born in 1962 and my youngest brother, Alain was born in 1967. When Alain was born, I was nine years old, in the Girl Guides and leading an interesting life. I treated him like my own baby. I would come home from school and look after him. On one occasion when I was twelve years old, after disagreeing obstinately with my father about a decision relating to Alain, he stopped me and explained that I was not his actual mother. I laugh when I remember that episode.

My parents were born five weeks apart in 1930 and considered themselves as equals and also treated all of us equally. We all had the same amount of chores, all took out the trash and all shoveled the winter snow; my brothers helped with the cooking and the cleaning. It was a beautiful way for my parents to raise a family. We five siblings were extremely close.

I shared a room with my sister. It was a magnificent bedroom with furniture made and decorated for us by our father. The walls were covered with pink and white-striped tapestry with a border of Cinderella carriages. We had princess-style beds. I loved spending time in our room - it was magical.

We were a middle class family and we always had all that we needed and much of what we wanted, such as new bicycles. We were the first family on the street to have a color television, a new oven and a microwave. I remember in about 1962, when I was about 4 years old, my mother appeared on a television show called Today's Women (Femmes D'aujourd' hui). I loved seeing her on television and believed that anybody can appear on television and that everything is possible. The local mayor lived in our street and, again, I thought that anybody can be a mayor because our neighbor was one. Instead of seeing a hierarchy of levels within a community, I felt that all people were equal and that everyone was accessible.

As my father was a travelling salesman, he was away much of the time. I admired him and loved spending time with him. He was tall and handsome and always wore a suit. He was very personable and seemed to know and speak to everyone we met. I inherited his personality and found it natural to be friendly and open with others. My father's company changed his car every year and when he arrived home in the new vehicle he would honk the horn and the entire family would run out to admire the new car.

We were raised as Catholics and went to church every Sunday in my father's car. On the Saturday night my mother would help us choose our clothes for church. We showered and polished our shoes so that we would not be rushing on Sunday morning. After mass, we would have lunch with my maternal grandmother Jeanne and then go to my other grandparents' house for dinner. We did this every Sunday. My paternal grandparents were Paul Chaloux and Lucille Therrien. I got along with all my grandparents. I believed we had an amazing family.

When my father went away for work, my mother was at home with us and grandmother Jeanne would come to stay with us during the week. We would take it in turns to sleep with our mother or grandmother. We loved sleeping in their beds and listening to their stories. At times, I would go to my grandmother's for the weekend and she would tell me stories of my great grandmother, Clara Bourgeois. I was fascinated to hear the stories. Great grandmother Clara lived in a huge apartment, above a row of shops. In one of the shops was a Chinese laundry that was run by two Chinese men who couldn't stay in the country very long as it was difficult for Chinese people to migrate to Quebec if they were not of the Catholic or Christian faith. The apartment had previously been her mother's home. There was a grand hotel situated opposite her home and many stars from Quebec came and stayed at the hotel, but that was well before I was born.

Over the years my parents were part of many organizations and they held meetings at our house. I remember my parents pushing the furniture aside and placing chairs in every available spot. I was only two when the meetings started. The purpose of the meetings was to bring estranged couples closer together and unite troubled families. I developed a strong belief that through meetings and discussions we could help others.

When my father started working as a salesman, he promised my mother that they would go away together twice a year to make up for the time that they spent apart. She agreed to that and they left twice a year, leaving us at home in the care of my grandmother and, at times, babysitters. We became more independent with each absence and enjoyed our time together. We quickly learnt how to survive on our own. At times we felt a little abandoned but we knew that we were in good hands and had someone to turn to. We rarely quarreled with each other which was quite unusual for five children. It was a happy period of our lives.

On one occasion, when I was about 9 years old we were left in the care of a female babysitter when my parents took a break and went on a cruise. Alain started crying because of an earache. Normally we would hug him to try and settle him but the babysitter told us to leave him alone and let him cry himself to sleep. My older brother and I felt that our youngest brother was in danger so we decided to get out of there. We caught two buses to reach my grandmother's house. When she came to the door, she found five of us staring up at her, telling her that we had run away from home. My brother Michel became my hero after this episode. I still don't know how he found the money for the bus to get us to our grandmother's house, but he did and we were so happy to see her.

Michel struggled over the years due to a cardiac malfunction when he was very young. He underwent open heart surgery at the age of twenty five and during the transfusion of blood, he was given infected blood from which he contracted Hepatitis C. Many times over the years he would have to go to hospital to treat his illness. I hated seeing him sick. I learnt so much from him and through his passion for the Beatles I discovered and developed a love for music.

My mother had one brother, Uncle Jacques. He is an important figure in my life as he is also my godfather and has always treated me like a daughter. With my parents, my grandmother Jeanne and my uncle Jacques, I felt that two mothers and two fathers raised us. He worked for Radio Canada and was a very cultured gay man. He knew a lot about everything because he travelled everywhere that he could in his spare time. From a very young age he taught us about music, history, different cultures and religions. At that time it was rare for people to travel to countries such as China and Russia but he had the confidence to leave and when he arrived at one destination, he made arrangements to go to the next destination. He brought us gifts of clothes, books and encyclopedias and shared his wealth of knowledge with us. We realized that we were extremely privileged children to learn about these things. I didn't hear of many people in Saint Jerome who travelled extensively during this time.

When I didn't know something, I would call him and he would

enlighten me. He took us to museums in Montreal and he continued to pass on his vast knowledge on a countless number of subjects. During my formative years, there were so many people around me that I trusted and respected and from whom I learnt so much about life. This is another reason why I developed into a person of strength and determination who is willing to find solutions to problems.

Our family life was perfect. I never saw my parents arguing and they were a loving couple towards each other. We always celebrated special occasions with our grandparents and there was always much affection showered on us, as well as many gifts. We received at least thirty presents at Christmas time and we enjoyed a life of abundance in all aspects. It was amazing and I felt so blessed. Even now that we are much older, we all see each other at least once a month for a birthday celebration or a special occasion.

In 1963 when I was five years old, I began primary school at the 'Convent of Good Advice' in Saint Jerome, an all girls' school run by nuns. This was the only school where white dresses were worn during the First Holy Communion ceremony. My mother refused to send me to a school where a uniform was worn for that ceremony. The school was chosen because of this issue.

We were living in Saint Antoine at the time and originally my neighbor was supposed to take me to school but he moved away from the neighborhood. At five years of age, before having learnt to read, I had no option but to take a bus to school on my own. I would put on my backpack and set off on my journey, catching one bus before transferring to a second bus and making my way to the school.

I got to know all the adults on the bus and they became my friends. It was the same on the return trip in the afternoon. One morning I saw my bus driver change buses so I followed him and sat on his bus because I trusted him. When I noticed that he wasn't following the usual route I started to cry because I didn't know where I was anymore. The bus driver told me not to cry and that he would take me to school. He changed his entire route and took me to school. That wonderful bus driver taught me that by having trust in people I would arrive at my intended destination.

The school was a boarding school but I lived close enough to live at home and commute. I got along well with girls in the grade above me and they took care of me as they would their younger sister. Sometimes I missed the bus on the way home and would sit and eat lunch with them in the school kitchen area. There was an aura of harmony and ease in that lunchroom and I really enjoyed being there. As I sat with the girls, I was inspired by places like this that brought people together in peace and love, with no confrontation.

I remained at that school for my first year until I was accepted at another Catholic primary school, 'Sainte Therese de L'Enfant Jesus' in Saint Antoine. As it was close to our house, I walked to school. The head nun was a deeply religious woman and I loved being at this school. I remained there for the next five years.

Throughout primary school, I would try to get to school early to help the teaching nuns. I would do their photocopying and help in whatever way I could. I owe a lot to these particular nuns as they were extremely inspiring. I made friends with them because at that point in time, I was convinced that I was going to be a nun. Ever since I was young, I had a strong belief that I was put on this earth to do my best, to live a good life and to help others. I believe in re-incarnation and I was convinced that I was born into this world to do good deeds. I thought the best way to do that would be to become a nun. As I sensed that I had tried to enter this life twice previously as a boy, but ended up coming as a girl, I felt that I was both sexes in one soul and didn't feel the need at the time to be in a relationship.

Whenever friends needed help, they were allowed to stay over so that I could cheer them up. In fact, all my brothers and sisters helped their friends. I had a good friend, Lizanne and we were the same height which means more on the shorter side. She was a very sporty girl but she had a lot of family issues. As her parents told her that they hadn't planned to have her and that she was an 'accident', she often felt rejected. She stayed over our house often and we participated in many activities and sports together throughout our school years.

My parents kept holding the meetings at our house with people from the community so between those sessions, catching the bus independently and the entire school experience with the nuns and other students, I started to define my goals for later life.

When I was five years old my father took me for a medical procedure because I kept having ear aches and my tonsils often became inflamed. We went to a specialized clinic where I had a tonsillectomy. I didn't understand what was happening at the time but my father held me securely in his arms and it felt like paradise to me. I was put under anesthetic and when I woke up, I had no idea of time. My father drove me home whilst I was still very drowsy and as he carried me inside I felt like a fuzzy doll in my father's arms. He was so strong and loving.

I remained at home for two weeks of recuperation and during that time my grandmother Jeanne took care of me.

My grandmother Jeanne with her headphones

It was during this period that she told me the fascinating stories of my great grandmother, her mother, Clara Bourgeois. I was so captivated by her stories that I continued having discussions with her for the next 30 years. I was the only child interested in hearing the stories. As I listened to the many tales about my great grandmother, I also developed an ability to analyze situations and find the best solution.

Even though my great grandmother Clara died in 1948, ten years before I was born, she was a major inspiration to me and I still sense a very strong connection to her. Although she was a midwife by profession, she also took care of the elderly and dying whilst looking after her own children. Clara's husband was the station master in the Saint Jerome region for more than 60 years. During her life, birth control was unheard of and as the Catholic Church encouraged women to have a child every year if possible, she ended up with seventeen children. She approached the bishop to annul her marriage on the grounds that she was physically related to her own husband. The bishop refused and told her to keep having children. Ever since hearing this story about the bishop, I knew that it was important for me to have a good relationship with any bishop that I dealt with so that I could speak openly and we could solve any problems mutually.

Clara was actively involved in Saint Jerome as she was on the Administration Council of three different religious orders of nuns. At the time, she was also president of the third Tier Order of St. Francis of Assisi, which doesn't exist anymore.

Every day, after making a huge cauldron of soup for her children, she would take some bowls of soup to the elderly and forgotten. In those days, many elderly residents lived in abandoned sheds at the back of some old houses. When anyone died, she washed their bodies and helped the family, if any, to grieve. She was a woman who dedicated her whole life to her family and community.

Back in those days, when a woman gave birth to a child, the other children left the house so as to not witness the birth. Usually they went to a barn close to the house, remained there until the birth and then went back inside to welcome the new baby. To explain the event, parents told their children that a Native Indian man had come, beat their mother and left her with a child. This story originated from events during the French colonization period of Canada. Many of the French men didn't have a wife and the church was against them marrying Native American women, even though many had inter-racial sexual relations. If a Native American woman gave birth to a 'white' child, the Native American chief would take the 'white' baby and leave it on the birth father's doorstep.

Near Clara's house was a trail used by the homeless which stretched from Saint Therese to Saint Adele via Saint Jerome. During their walk, the homeless would stop at Clara's house. She had a bench inside her home where they could rest, sleep, and eat.

One cold winter day, a homeless woman with holes in her socks and boots stopped at the house. Clara knew that there was no way the woman could walk the track to Saint Adele without her toes freezing. She went to a metal box in the cupboard and took out the family savings. Some of the family told her not to take the money as there would be none left for them to buy food. Clara replied "No, today God wants us to respond to the urgent needs of this person so we must do just that". She went and bought the women some new socks and boots and after expressing her enormous gratitude, the woman continued on her journey.

Later that day, Clara's husband arrived home from work with a package from Saint Veronique, a township further north in the Laurentians region. Many years previously, during the colonization period, Father Antoine Labelle (Curé Labelle), a Roman Catholic priest had asked families to help purchase land so that the money could be used to develop the road further north into the Laurentians region. Clara's family helped him by purchasing terrains in Sainte Veronique. The road was developed and then many years later, the owners could sell their lands. The parcel that arrived that same afternoon contained the final paperwork regarding the sale of these terrains that her family had bought. Clara was now going to be wealthy. With a great sense of happiness and relief she said to her children, "You see, if you help in the right places, God arranges everything so that things work out well".

Her eldest daughter disagreed and told her that even if she hadn't helped that woman, they would still have received the money. Clara said, "No, if we hadn't helped that woman, we wouldn't have received that money. Everything is linked". This story taught me to concentrate on what is happening in the present. If I do something major to help someone today, it is a great day and tomorrow may be even better.

There was another story about one of the local shopkeepers. He had a big problem with mice. Clara told him that if he wanted to get rid of his mice problem, he should sell his mice to the homeless woman and she would get rid of them. She never explained how she would do it so he didn't believe her but agreed. Clara gave the homeless woman the money to pay him and the mice disappeared and went north with the woman. The store owner was so relieved and extremely happy with Clara's suggestion. There is similar children's story about a man, his flute and mice but this is our local legend about Clara.

My grandmother Jeanne was one of Clara's seventeen children and she was the child who lived the longest. She only had two children, my mother and my uncle Jacques because she became sterile at the age of 37. She wanted more children but couldn't have any more. She was an amazing grandmother, more like a sister or a friend. We spent lots of time together and she never once needed to be authoritarian with me.

Three of grandmother Jeanne's sisters were nuns so I had three great aunts who were nuns (pictured above). Their names were Febrenie,

Aurore and Blanche. My grandmother was very happy to spend time with them and although she was a very pious woman, she didn't want to be a nun. The three sisters often came to our house for Christmas and Easter. They were generous, kind women and I admired them greatly. They were a big presence in my life and part of the reason why I wanted to be a nun. In the many group photos I have of them, there is a person who looks like me in the picture with them, but it's actually my mother. My mother and I are very alike.

One of the nuns took care of an orphanage, the other took care of the sick and the third travelled the world as a missionary. They were inspirational in all their accomplishments and their constant energy stream. Their brother Henry found a porcelain figurine of three nuns and bought three for the sisters' family. When the first sister, Febrenie died in 1966, Henry painted their names on the back of one of the figurines (pictured below) and gave it to my grandmother.

I inherited the figurine. It really is a beautiful representation of them. The second nun, Sister Aurore died in 1970 and Sister Blanche a few years after that. The three of them taught me how it was possible to expand one's horizon and accomplish extraordinary things.

My grandmother Jeanne loved to paint and created some fine artworks when she was young. Her works included historical portraits of Native Americans, one of sick children, another of a woman and her dog, and one of Napoleon on Saint Helena's Island in the Atlantic Ocean where he was exiled. I have a few of her paintings in my home.

She stopped painting when she got married in 1928. She explained to me that when she was young, she fell in love with a man whose father was an alcoholic and her parents refused to allow them to marry, stating that alcoholism was hereditary and that he would become one in turn. As she was still not married at the age of twenty eight and was not interested in being with another man, her parents gave her the ultimatum of either getting married or becoming a nun. The family introduced her to a man soon afterwards. She didn't get to know him very well and he wasn't the love of her life but they were married. She had children immediately with him and spent her time raising the children and working in his stores and hence gave up her painting. I never met her husband as he died a few months before I was born.

A painting by my grandmother Jeanne

One day, my father took all the family and grandmother Jeanne to Mont–Laurier where he rented a chalet. When she was with us children, she always had a smile on her face and laughed all the time. We were sitting at the table and about to drink some freshly made fruit juice when it spilt all over the table. Grandmother Jeanne looked around to see if my parents were watching and then she took a straw and slurped it straight off the table. We laughed so much with her. She was, at the one time, the pillar of the family, a big sister and a joker playing tricks on us.

She was very creative and she loved to sew. If I wanted a new dress, I would draw it on paper and she would make it for me. I watched her and learnt to sew at the same time. She also taught me how to draw and paint.

My grandmother lived with her sister Imelda for many years later in life. I remember my sister and me discussing the possibility of living together when we were older because we saw what a wonderful experience it was for them. They were very close, just as I am with my sister.

The first death I experienced in my life was in 1964 when I was nearly seven years old. My paternal grandfather had been at work and when he came home, he found my grandmother Lucille deceased in her bed. Someone told us that wolf prints had been found on the window ledge of her room. We believed that wolves had come to get her but, in reality, she died of a heart attack. It was a tough time for all of us when my father lost his mother because we were a close family. I remember crying at school the next day and my teacher telling me to stop. She told me that we shouldn't cry when we lose our grandmothers. I thought that the teacher didn't love anybody because when you love someone, it is normal to feel sadness. I no longer got to see my grandmother Lucille on Sundays for dinner and no longer enjoyed her company at New Year's Eve parties.

The night before the funeral we held the first service at the funeral home. The casket was open so that we could all say our goodbyes. When my little sister tried to kiss my grandmother on the cheek, she toppled into the casket. We stood there in shock, looking at each other in disbelief before running to lift my sister out of the casket. I can laugh about it now but, at the time, everyone was in mourning and in a very somber mood. There were many children there and being typical children, we played hide and seek at the funeral home all day.

Her funeral was held at the church and we all attended and shed many tears during the service. We firmly believed that our grandmother had gone to heaven because she was such a good woman. I remember my father saying that he wanted to die quickly, like she had done, when he reached 64 because he didn't want anyone to take care of him.

I remember playing with around twenty-five of the local neighborhood kids on the river near our house. On this particular day, the weather was warmer than usual. We were playing on the ice when, all of a sudden, it gave way and we all fell into the water. Luckily, the water wasn't very deep in that spot so we broke out into laughter. However when we climbed out some of the other children stopped laughing. They became very scared because some thought they would be grounded whilst others believed that they would get a beating from their parents. I tried to explain to them that it wasn't their fault that they got wet but that didn't really help them. I wasn't afraid of anybody. Perhaps for one moment I thought I was afraid of the Pope but, in reality, not even His Holiness scared me. No one was going to stop me from doing what I wanted to do.

I inherited that attitude from my mother, a devout Catholic woman who was very involved in many benevolent associations as well as being part of the school council and the school commission. Even now, at the age of 83, she volunteers to read the bible and give communion at church. She always reminds me that nobody told her what to do. Both my parents also never made promises that they couldn't keep.

When I was nine years old, my parents organized to take my brothers and me to an international exhibition (Expo 67) in Montreal. My mother was pregnant with Alain at the time and my sister Marie Josée was still too young at the time to come with us. It was the time when the Metro was first opened and no-one knew how it worked. We got to the station platform and when the train came in and the doors opened, my mother walked inside with Michel and Pierre and the doors closed behind them. My father and I were left standing on the platform, looking at them inside the train. As the train started moving away, my father frantically tried to signal my mother. I thought that I had lost my mother that day. My father got us onto another train and we met up with them a little while later. Our first experience on the Metro was a fiasco but nevertheless, a funny experience.

Chapter XII

In 1969, the government decided to build an airport in Mirabel. The government expropriated our homes, in other words, seized our property through a compulsory purchase. The displaced were able to rent their homes from the government but many people decided to move away from the area as they didn't know what would happen next. I lost many friends during that time as their families moved away.

We didn't want to move so we stayed in our home and rented it from the government. The government told us that the new airport would create jobs in the area. I thought that if I could one day get a job at the airport, it would be beneficial to speak several languages and decided to concentrate on learning some other languages.

In 1971, I began secondary school at Frenette. In the previous year, due to an educational restructure, some students with high grades missed the 7th year of primary school and went directly to secondary school. My mother felt that I was too young to leave primary school and didn't allow me to skip the level as did many of my friends. I was very disappointed with her decision and it was a difficult time for me being a year behind my friends.

My mother was on the council of the school commission and, at that time, the education system was undergoing serious changes. Many priests and nuns stopped teaching and lay teachers took over. I was at a new school with new rules and secondary school was split into three stages, each at different locations. For one year, I was at the first school at which there were very rigid guidelines for school attire. One day my mother told me that a decision had been made at the school commission meeting to relax the clothing regulations. The following day I went to school in hot pants and my teacher shouted at me and sent me to the school principal's office. He told me that I was not allowed to wear hot pants to school. I told him that I could as a decision had been made to allow greater flexibility. I felt so proud of myself for knowing about this change in policy before others in authority and I teased them on this point.

My principal made some calls and realized that I was telling the truth - I got to wear my hot pants at school. I wasn't afraid to knock down closed doors. Once they made the decision at the council, I simply implemented the policy immediately.

In the following year, 1972, I went to Marchand School. I devoted myself to playing sports. I trained before and after school and competed in the regional competitions doing the asymmetric bars in gymnastics and the obstacle course.

I came first in our region of Saint Jerome and was sent to compete in the provincial Quebec Championships. I came fourth in these events but as that meant that I did not win any award or appear on the podium, I felt humiliated. As all my hard work didn't achieve any great results I decided to stop concentrating on sport completely as it wasn't worth my time.

From 1973 I attended the Polyvalent School for secondary years three, four and five. My brother Michel was also at that school in year five and all his friends welcomed me and kept on eye out on me. I was their little protégé. I loved the care and attention bestowed on me and felt privileged that I ate my meals and had fun with them all.

New neighbors moved into our street and I kept noticing a young man called Normand. We became friends and my father invited him over for dinner quite often. He was gay but we didn't care. He became a big part of our family and we loved having him around. To this day, we are very close and visit each other often.

My father wanted my brother Pierre to follow in his footsteps and join the army. He said it was good for discipline. I was furious at his decision because I had just spent three days on a hunger strike in a park in Saint Jerome, protesting against the sending of troops to the Vietnam War. The bishop supported our strike and came to check up on us to make sure that we didn't die of hunger. We displayed slogans promoting world peace. I was fourteen at the time and angry with my father because I didn't want my brother to be sent to war because of what I considered to be a stupid decision by USA politicians. It was my opinion that we needed to promote love and peace in the world, not war.

1974 was a different year for me at school as Michel and the boys had all left. Michel began working for a company that made electrical wire and ended up marrying a lovely girl. Not many people were getting married at that time. I was not sure if I was going to get married because I still wanted to be a nun. I was quite confused because as I was looking after my brother Alain after school, I thought it would also be nice to have children of my own one day. I knew that I couldn't marry and be a nun at the same time. We were hearing about many females having abortions at that time and I couldn't understand why that was happening. At school, I wrote an essay about a foetus that had been aborted and its spirit went through a severe depression because someone had refused to allow it to live. Hearing all this debate about abortion confirmed my desire to have children of my own.

With the change in my previously social lunch breaks, I devoted my time to more responsible interests such as the World Youth Council and Youth of the World (Jeunes Du Monde). They were separate but similar organizations. We were involved in many pastoral activities for students at the school and also planned trips away with our friends to meet other young people from all around the world. One of the groups originated from the village of *Taizé* in France where the St Francis of Assisi church was located. They started the World Youth Council and set up branches in Saint Jerome, Quebec City, Sherbrooke and New York. The students came together to pray and to try and find solutions as to how they could improve the world.

My participation opened many doors for me as well as giving me the opportunity to create some wonderful friendships. The young priests at our school also created a movement to bring many Catholic student groups together. We assembled together in an allocated room to organize activities. One of the annual events was a fundraiser called 'Walk for the Third World' and all the money raised was distributed to third world countries.

One other time, we created a giant mural for the school. We met in a room, started the music and painted. It was a very positive and vibrant environment. There was always a priest with us so that we weren't jeered or demotivated by any criticism or negativity.

In the winter, another Christian group called 'The Four Seasons' was formed. This group was based on outdoor activities. On one occasion, the group accompanied by one of the priests, all wearing snow shoes, hiked through the Mt Tremblant area. There were two full busloads of youth that set off to hike in the woods. These were extremely constructive and bonding outings.

My first trip away with my friends Francine, Lyne, and Marianne was to Quebec City in 1974. It was for the 'la Superfrancofête' (Super French Celebration). It was an international get-together for young people. I was sixteen at the time and we told our parents that we would stay on Île d'Orléans. We were heading there on the bus but en route we decided to get off at Quebec City and camp on the actual site of the fête. When we arrived we were told there was no camping permitted on 'Les Plaines D'Abraham' (Abraham's Plains). As we had nowhere to stay we thought we would be homeless for a few days. A lady noticed us and invited us to camp in her backyard, right near the site. We pitched our tents and felt much more secure until it began to rain so heavily that everything was soaked. We ran for cover under the university buildings nearby and found some underground corridors. This was the only dry place where we could sleep. It was an incredible adventure and we had a lot of fun. We didn't need alcohol or drugs to enjoy ourselves.

It was pure, clean fun.

I had many wonderful friends over the years such as Francine, Marianne and Chantal. Francine lived in the same area and decided to change her name to Colombine. She ended up leaving for Europe and when she came back, many years later, she was married to a man from France. I don't see her very often now. My friend Marianne and I worked at the school auditorium as we loved music and it was our way to see music shows together for free. We were volunteers and we loved being able to meet the artists after their performance. We felt very privileged. Marianne came from a big family, loved to paint and we had a lot in common.
Chantal lived in Saint Janvier and she was the youngest of a big family of girls. I envied her a little as her older sisters taught her so much and I didn't have an older sister.

On another trip we went to New York for the World Youth Council and met people from all over the world. The purpose of the event was to develop a greater understanding of others and develop strategies for helping others. We completed many activities that were aimed at breaking down prejudices. On our first day we were put in a team with a person from a different culture, religion, skin color and language. I was teamed with an African Protestant boy. We spent the whole day together and openly discussed anything and everything. These experiences were very unifying and enriching.

We undertook many more trips to different places and it was a great period in my life.

In 1975, I enrolled in drama classes at school and became part of the improvisation group. Another member of our group was Robert, whom I considered to be the cutest boy in the class. One of our tasks during the summer period was to develop a project and perform at various points around Quebec. My father didn't want me to go, knowing that Robert would also be going. I explained that the whole group would be there but that didn't matter to him. He said I was too young to be going away on such a trip. I didn't like the idea of having limitations imposed on me so I thought that if I got married, I could have the freedom I desired.

My parents left for Mexico that summer on one of their trips. My father was having problems with his pulmonary artery and it was beneficial for him to spend some time in a warmer climate, relaxing by the beach and taking in the sea air. In early 1976, whilst my parents were away in Mexico, Robert and I decided to get married. I was seventeen years old when he asked me to marry him but eighteen when we actually got married. My parents didn't believe that we were getting married but a week after they returned from Mexico, we were married. My father asked me if I wanted money for a church wedding or money for the honeymoon. I decided on the church wedding to thank him for everything that he had given me in life.

We had the service at Saint Antoine Catholic Church on the 6th March, 1976. I wore a beautiful white dress with a big fur cape because it was still very cold. Being so young, I looked as if it were my first Holy Communion rather than my wedding. The wedding reception was an elaborate lunch for the entire family. It was a lovely family day. We had rented a lovely honeymoon suite in Val David for the night. We got lost trying to find the place as a big snowstorm had hit that day and was still raging as we left the reception center. We couldn't find the venue so we rented a small room in a motel.

It was a happy time for me because it was the beginning of a new life. We had finished school but didn't have a graduation ball with my friends because the teachers went on strike at the end of the school year. It was as if we never formally finished high school – our school days just ended.

Robert and I moved into an apartment in Saint Jerome. I was the first of my friends to get married and felt a little estranged from them. My friend Lyne moved away to Vancouver; some others moved to the city to advance their studies and careers.

I fell pregnant in the following year. Everyone was very happy for us because they all knew how much I wanted a baby. My brother Michel already had one child so I looked after him at the apartment whilst Robert went to work at Lumen Electrical.

One night we were in bed fast asleep and I awoke feeling very strange. My contractions were two minutes apart. Robert called a taxi to take us to the hospital and in his excitement, paid the taxi driver almost double the fare. By the time we got to the hospital, the baby was on its way. The nurse told me to stop pushing because she needed to get the doctor to inject me with an epidural. In 1977 it was mandatory to have an epidural even though I didn't want one. I told the nurse that I couldn't stop as the baby's head was almost out. I could see the baby's black hair. The doctor rushed in and gave me the epidural at the same time as the baby was born. It was a very smooth birth and I didn't feel much pain at all.

I was so happy looking at my first born child. I kept on thinking that it was impossible for me to give birth to something so perfect. It felt miraculous to have been blessed with a child. We named him Mathieu and I started breast feeding him straight away. I was in the hospital for three days until we went back to the apartment.

My younger brother Pierre was still attending the Polyvalent School and would come over at lunch times and play with the baby. It was a joyful time. At times I felt like a child with a child. I was only nineteen years old and I loved my life.

A friend told me that she was pregnant but wasn't ready for a child. She didn't want an abortion either so she finally decided to put the baby up for adoption. She asked me about the pain during the birth and I told her it was fine for me and quite easy. Her labor was so tough on her that she rang me afterwards saying that I was totally wrong and had lied to her as she had a very bad labor and had suffered terribly. I remember laughing about that. Luckily, I didn't have that experience.

Robert and I were approached by a man we knew to look after his home rent-free. He had a farmhouse that the government had bought from him and which he had subsequently rented back. As he still had a lease on the house he needed someone to live there to make sure that no-one stole any of the farming equipment or possessions whilst he was away. We decided that this was a great opportunity and moved in when Mathieu was nine months old. It was a big house near the woods in Marguerite Lane, Mirabel. There were fields all around the house and our backyard was one kilometer deep. I loved being there and frequently visited my parents in Saint Antoine.

Mathieu and I at Cavendish in 1978

My brother Michel had baptized his children. I debated whether to baptize Mathieu as I didn't fully trust the particular priest at the time and didn't want him to do anything strange to my child. I chose not to have Mathieu baptized.

It wasn't long before I became pregnant with my second child and by 30th August, 1979, I was heavily pregnant and the baby was overdue. It was as if the child didn't want to come out. We went to the doctor and he told us that I was 5cms dilated and should start preparing for the new arrival. We went home, packed our suitcases and dropped Mathieu off at my parents' home in Saint Antoine. Robert drove me to the hospital and the doctor began to induce labor and start the contractions. It was a long and very painful process. I suffered a lot during this pregnancy and I kept thinking about what my friend had told me about her painful labor. I now totally understood.

I gave birth to my second beautiful boy. He was perfect and worth every moment of pain. We named him Jérémé and I loved looking after both my baby boys. I wanted to keep having children but early in 1980 I went to see the doctor as I wasn't feeling well. He told me that I had the same medical issues as my grandmother and that I wouldn't be able to have any more children. I was devastated and it also meant that I would have to go through a painful operation that would render me sterile. As distraught as I was by the news, I kept telling myself that I could adopt more children in the future.

At the end of the formal lease on the house, the lease-holder did not wish to renew the government lease because he had purchased land elsewhere in Bellefeuille. He needed to find a farmer for his new lease as the land was classified as agricultural farmland. We were not eligible to take on this lease as we weren't farmers. I panicked at the thought of moving and went to my parents' house in Saint Antoine to share the news with them. Across from their house was another that I loved and used to visit in my childhood. It always had a particular energy about it. It had a soul and I dreamt of living in that house. It is in this house that I still live.

These particular houses were bought out many years before by the government and were now managed by the Canadian Estate Agency. The former owners stayed on in their homes under a lease agreement. I went to speak to the gardener at the house, who lived on the premises. He was a lovely man and he looked after the farm animals and all the rare trees that were planted around the house by the original owner. I told him about our situation and explained that I would love to live in that house.

The gardener called me soon afterwards to tell me that he had to move away to Saint Sophie because he was no longer allowed to have farm animals in that area of Saint Jerome. I asked him not to tell the Agency that he was moving as I wanted it for my family. He agreed and the lease remained in his name. I moved into the house with Robert, my children and my brother Pierre. A few months later, I went to the Canadian Estate Agency, informed them that I was the occupier of the house and that I needed a new lease. They told me "No, you're not allowed to be there, you will have to leave".

They explained that there was a waiting list of municipality councilors and police officers etc, and that it was impossible for me to lease the house. I told them that it was not my fault that the government had evicted my parents from our family home and that they had an obligation to relocate me, having been a juvenile victim of their action. I told them that I found the house and that I would stay in it. They put a lot of pressure on us to move out but as my father was heavily involved in politics at the time, he met with the deputy and made arrangements for us to stay on in the house. Six months later, we had our lease. Pierre lived with us for one year at the house.

In that same year, 1980, I was still eager to have more children and came up with the idea of opening a day care center at my house. That way I could look after my children and work at the same time. It was a great idea and I was able to work and save some money for the future.

Mathieu was three years old at that time and he had a little box in his room where he put all his precious items. I asked him why he had such a small box. He turned to me and said, "It's because in the army, we can't have much stuff".

He was only three years old and his comment upset me greatly. I told him that I didn't give birth to him so he could join the army and be killed. He responded with conviction, "Sorry, I will join the army. Sorry mummy, it's my life".

In the following year, 1981, I became involved in Youth House, an organization which helped troubled teenagers. I spent a lot of time with one young teenage girl and realized that I needed to learn more about the problematic issues that these young people faced. I decided to enroll in university and study Psychosocial Intervention.

In 1982, I was accepted by the University of Quebec in Montreal (UQAM). I looked after the children during the day and studied at night. Luckily there was a campus in Saint Jerome which meant I could study locally rather than travelling to Montreal.

In 1983, my paternal grandfather died. He became very sick and couldn't eat but I don't exactly remember the cause of his death. I was glad that he didn't suffer for very long. It was a sad time for the entire family. On the night of his death, my grandfather came and spoke to me in a dream. He told me that he wanted us to save the park of the 'little river Saint Antoine' for the sake of lost souls. He explained that there were souls of deceased persons lingering around which couldn't go back into the light and they needed a place to reflect and accept that they were deceased. That park was the last piece of untouched wilderness in Saint Jerome and it was important to keep it as a place of refuge.

That was around the time when the government made all the lands that they expropriated available for repurchase by the original owners. Parks would remain the property of the government. My parents were among those that bought back their home. The city of Saint Antoine bought the park and wanted to turn it into an industrial zone.

I went to see the city council with a request to protect the park. I was told that the plans had been submitted to build the industrial zone, to divert the river and redirect the water through an underground pipe. As the zoning of the area would need to be changed,, the public can take part in the redevelopment consultation process. We could submit our objections or support and I lodged my objections. I listed many arguments opposing the development. The main argument was that it was the last sizable public site in the area and that the nearest river was in the next council region. I provided traffic reports and explained that there were six lanes of traffic on the road next to the park and that there had been several fatalities at the corner of the park because of the busy road.

I explained that if they demolished the park, my children, as well as all other children, would have to cross that very busy road to get to another park which was much further away. I suggested that the council wouldn't want to be responsible for the death of children. I was invited to present my concerns in person. When I arrived at the council meeting, I was accompanied by twelve, sweet, innocent-looking children. The councilors couldn't stop staring at them during the session. They listened to my views and it felt good to have a voice.

Several years after that council meeting, in 1992 the area was re-zoned and turned into a protected park. We had a massive victory and I knew my grandfather was with me every step of the way. It is now a wonderful community park with beautiful gardens and walking trails. Over the years we have held many community events at that park with local Native American people. Safe spots were created for small outdoor fires so that people could come and socialize. We held sacred fire lighting ceremonies and every time the Native Americans lit a fire, eagles came and flew above the fire until it was put out. It was an amazing sight and the eagles only came when the Native Americans were there.

I believe that I inherited my social commitment and sense of community responsibility from my great grandmother. I have always been inspired to fight for causes and find solutions to issues of this kind.

After my grandfather died, I decided to join my parents in Mexico. The boys and I left for Acapulco. One sunny day the boys were playing in the sand and my father and I were sitting on the sun chairs relaxing. My father called the waiter and asked for a Corona. I was in shock. I couldn't believe that my father was having a beer. I had never seen him drink before and I said to the waiter "Same here, same here".

Our beers arrived and we laughed and chatted and had a wonderful time together. During our one month holiday, I saw my father transform from a serious, mature man with a job, responsibilities and a mortgage into a carefree adolescent, treating me like a friend and joking with his buddies. My children loved spending time with my parents on our holiday. It was so special. We made many trips over the years to join them and each time it was a wonderful experience.

Our home-life had always been happy with a few straightforward rules. My father labeled it a dry house and no one drank alcohol. My grandfather had had a problem with alcohol and when my father got married, he made a pact with my grandfather that neither would ever touch alcohol again. They both honored that deal and we never saw either of them drink. Having a beer with my father in Mexico was a way of saluting my grandfather's memory.

Chapter XIII

When Jérémé started primary school in 1984, I decided to start a day care center at his school so that I could be closer to both of my boys during the day and concentrate on my university studies at night. The day care centers were very successful and I was able to save a good amount of money. Apart from the financial benefit, I really enjoyed looking after children.

In 1986, I took our family to Vancouver, BC, Canada for the World Exposition on Transportation and Communication, known as Expo '86. It was held from 2nd May until 13th October 1986 on the north shore of False Creek. The Canadian government invested CAD $311 million to set up the exposition and it was a huge success in terms of attracting tourism to Canada even though it put the country into financial deficit. These major world expositions are held in different countries every few years with the focus on a different theme of relevance to the world. (Expo 2015 was held in Milan, Italy – *'Feeding the planet, Energy for life'*.)

Although we stayed with my friend Lyne, it was a costly trip for us because of travel expenses and the cost of tickets at the Expo. The tickets were $30 each per day so for our family of four, it was $120 per day. There was so much to see and do as most countries from around the world were represented as well as many global organizations. I was greatly inspired and wanted to stay longer to see more of the exhibition but it was too expensive.

On the third day, we were queuing up to enter a pavillion when we began chatting with an elderly man who was part of a group of 70 people from Quebec. He told us that they all had tickets for three days but that many of the older people couldn't cope with the distances and size of the exposition. The man told me that he was leaving the following morning at 6am and that he would try to get us some unused tickets. We arranged to meet him the next morning and when I arrived at 5.30am he gave me 90 tickets for free to use during the entire exposition. I couldn't believe it.

We gave some tickets to Lyne and her sister's families and used the remainder going in and out of the exposition until we saw everything that we wanted to see.

I noticed the pavillion for the United Nations (UN) and once inside, I spotted the stand for the UN High Commissioner for Refugees (UNHCR). I was studying psychosocial intervention and this was the first time that I could truly relate my studies to the issues faced by refugees. I was so excited to be there and after long discussions with the representatives, it was becoming very clear to me as to what I wanted to do in life. I wanted to work for the UN to help refugees.

I was so grateful that we were able to attend Expo '86 and that I had discovered exactly what it was that I wanted to do in the future. The whole experience changed my life. If it wasn't for the generous elderly man, I would not have been able to spend as much time in the UN pavillion, talking with all the representatives and establishing my principal focus points. I purchased a big poster from the UN tent and had it laminated. Unfortunately it was stolen a few years ago from my office so I only have an image from the internet to remember those wonderful moments.

I applied to work with the United Nations immediately and they contacted me saying that instead of working for the UN directly, it would be more advantageous if I could set up an organization in my area that could assist refugees. That would assist the UN in finding places for refugees to settle. I would need to ensure that the location complied with all regulations and had social services in place to handle the arrival of refugees in the area. I was motivated by that suggestion.

In the interim, I decided to apply to the Employment Search Centre for the Laurentians region, known as CREL. It was an organization that provided training to people that wanted to go back into the workforce. This particular cooperative of workers constituted a great team. The team was autonomous and independent and all were very respected individuals within the local community. They worked together extraordinarily and were able to face many challenges in order to find successful solutions. I was proud to be a part of that team and enjoyed the extremely stimulating workplace. I worked at

CREL from 1988 to 1991.

During that same time, between 1987 and 1990, the National Society of Quebec (La Société Nationale des Québécois) formed and conducted a study over three years through team consultations on the demographic development of the Laurentians region. I was part of this organization and we identified different trends that were occurring. We noted that there was a reduction in births and that we had an aging population. We discussed immigration trends within the country and between 1987–1988 we completed many reports on these topics and presented them at various conferences. I was filmed presenting my reports and I was able to share my vision with others. I explained how immigrants were coming to visit the Laurentians but were unable to remain because there was no organization or established facility where they had access to services which would help with their integration into our society.

At the same time the federal government signed a treaty which declared the province of Quebec as responsible for the Provincial Immigration Policy. The federal government wanted to develop an alliance among its regions so that they could work together to apply new immigration policies. We examined the regionalization of immigration in great length and it was through these discussions that the idea came to me of opening a center for immigrants with the purpose of retaining immigrants in our region. I knew that through this center I could begin to work with the UN and organize to bring refugees into our area and integrate them into society. This is how the Coffret was conceived and how I became the director of the center.

During 1988, I remember visiting a friend in Gaspesie and sitting by the ocean with a group of people. Many of them were recently separated and it seemed that divorce was becoming a trend. It was sad because many of the divorces were the result of extra-marital affairs which rarely lasted a long time. It didn't take long before many missed the stability that they had enjoyed in their previous relationships. Although I thought Robert and I had a happy and healthy relationship, we divorced around this time. I was in a state of total shock and disbelief.

Our children were nine and seven at the time and it was hard on them too. My parents were extremely upset because my brother Pierre and I were going through a divorce at the same time.

Thanks to my father I was, and am, by nature a very optimistic person and, at that time, I rarely got angry or screamed at anyone. It was a difficult and challenging time for the children and me. I couldn't believe what had happened to us but I needed to remain strong and move forward.

I kept feeling a need to have more children. I was drawn towards adoption over the years with many failed attempts. My father wanted to help me and we discussed going to Mexico to try and adopt a child from there. Once there, we went together to the adoption center and I completed the paperwork but was advised by the government agency that the policy is that two parents are required to adopt.

My father and I in Acapulco, Mexico 1988

I decided to try and adopt in Africa. I completed the paperwork and attached a photo to the application. I had very little energy during this period that I was supposed to leave. I was at home recovering from a surgical procedure and still had not renewed my passport. My father took my paperwork and went to Montreal on my behalf. My document was rejected because I was wearing a bandana in the photo. My father came back home, obtained another photo of me and tried again but the application was rejected again. My father was a constant source of support and always helped me in every way that he could.

We also tried to adopt in Chile and that didn't work out either. I guess it was the universe telling me that I needed to move forward in other ways.

Around this time, I decided that it would be a good idea for us to go to Europe. The school had organized for thirty children between the ages of seven and ten to participate in a student exchange program in France. I thought it was a wonderful opportunity for the children and decided that I would also go at the same time. It was a good escape for me and it would help to get my mind off the divorce. I was the only adult on the plane with all these children and even though I was not responsible for the other children, it was good to be with them and we all had a lot of fun. On arrival, my children headed for Paris and I decided to visit a friend who worked at the Château des Coudreaux in Chateaudun, in the Central Loire Valley. I met with the owner and she asked me to stay and work for her during my short stay. After the ten days, she begged me to stay permanently and for a moment, I seriously considered staying on as I would be close to the United Nations in Paris. However, I took my young children into account and decided that I would return to Quebec and pursue my personal goals there until my children were older.

I said my goodbyes and left for Paris. I so enjoyed exploring this beautiful city. I met up with my boys and the other children on the last two days. We visited the Louvre Museum in Paris and the children took photos of themselves beside the stunning monuments. Some of them tried to hang off the monuments. They really enjoyed the trip but I found that they were still too young at that age to really appreciate the whole experience. Upon our return, they mostly spoke of the house that they stayed in, and didn't like, as opposed to the entire adventure and the wonderful opportunity of discovering a new country and different culture. Overall, the trip was a success and we all had lots of fun.

When we returned, there was a crisis taking place in Oka, Saint Eustache. I read in the news that a policeman had been killed by a Native American. I knew there had to be more to this story and the more I thought about it, the more I realized that I didn't know enough about my indigenous ancestors. They were here before European migration and that is why we refer to them as people of the First Nation. I asked the universe for help in understanding their situation because I could feel there was a problem within their culture.

In 1989 and 1990, I completed a Certificate in Immigration and Intercultural Relations at Montreal University. At the first lesson, the entire lecture theatre was full and many students could not find a place to sit. The director of the University Program came forward and explained that a mistake had been made and too many students were accepted in that subject. Everyone was required to explain why they wanted to be in the class. The response given determined who would remain. I explained that I was the director of the Coffret and that I work directly with immigrants and needed this course in order to become more effective. There was a man standing behind me and he explained that he was from the First Nations and he needed to do this course because his community were having a problem with white people. I realized that the universe was answering my request. I had to talk to this man.

We were both accepted into the session and there was considerable team work activity. Apart from me, nobody wanted to work with that man. I had a lot to learn and he was my first contact with someone from the First Nations. He was from the Iroquois warrior clan. There are many different types of clans within the first nations and I met with him on many occasions over those two years to understand their background and current situation. He was a warrior by nature and always at war within himself about some matter. Eventually, I had to distance myself from him because I couldn't deal with the constant conflict.

On one occasion, he told to me about the cold war between Russia and the USA and how they had signed a treaty to disarm, making promises to the International Security Committee that they would stop the cold war. He told me that Russia had sold many of their weapons to Africans. People in the USA had managed to acquire these weapons and re-sell them. He claimed that his clan had got a hold of these weapons. I couldn't cope with hearing all this talk about people with weapons. I began to realize that I needed to associate with Native American mothers from various clans to understand my origins and hear less of these stories of war.

I have always enjoyed being amongst the trees and nature. Even in the winter months, I take my snow shoes and walk through the woods. I always felt connected to this land, especially to this region and I knew that I needed to explore the connection more. I often dreamt of reaching an old age and wandering through the woods, sleeping by a lake in a yurt (Mongol tent).

During that same course of study, I met a man who was a Messianic Jew. He was from Moldavia and was the first I had ever met from that country and that religion. I wanted to know more about his religion. I believed that if I could learn about the different religions in the world, it would help me in my desire to try and bring different religious groups together to discuss ways to move forward as a united entity. I asked him to explain his religion and to tell me about his country.

He told me what was happening to the children of Moldavia. When parents did not have enough money to feed their children, they took them to an orphanage and abandoned them. There was no one working at the orphanages so many of the children starved to death. He told me that it would be wonderful to try and come up with a way to have the children adopted before they died. I had tried to adopt children for many years and thought that this was an omen. I found a lawyer in Montreal and enlisted other people who had an interest in organizing adoptions of Moldavian orphans. In order to succeed in a venture of this kind, an accredited organization needs to be established and sanctioned by the government.

We finally held our first team meeting and the man bought a friend from Moldavia along to the meeting. They introduced themselves to the group. We came up with the strategy for gaining government accreditation and the selection criteria for potential adoptive parents. There was a large amount of paperwork to complete but I was certain that I could do it. After listening to us, one of the men from Moldavia stood up and said, "You don't have to do these papers. We take a boat and we take the children to the boat, we sail to Montreal through Saint Laurent and we give you a child for $25,000 each".

Shivers ran down my spine when I realized that they wanted to sell the children. Who were these people? They went on to say that they would bring boat loads of children to us every month. In their minds, the money earned would help their country. It was as if they were exporting fruit and vegetable crops or any other commodity. But these were children, not crops. It was an insane idea and I was ashamed in front of all present to have brought these two men before them. I immediately brought the entire project to an end.

There are many countries where orphaned children have had an extremely traumatized start in life. I have worked with families who have adopted children from various regions in Russia. The children are great in the first year whilst getting used to their new surroundings. Once they have adapted, their painful and disturbing experiences come back to haunt them and they turn into different children. They start to act in dangerous ways and psychiatric intervention is needed for these disturbed children from Russia. It becomes virtually impossible for these children to have a successful integration and unfeasible for Canada to accept more Russian children. It is an intolerable situation for the children, the families who adopt them and the hospitals that have to treat them.

In countries such as Cambodia and Thailand, children experience similar traumas but they seem to adapt more easily into new environments without obvious psychiatric disorders and I wander if it is resilience or genetics that determine the outcome.

By the late 1980's my grandmother Jeanne was living in a nursing home and in the early 1990's my sister Marie-Josée gave birth to her son Pier Oliver. I often visited them both.

During this period of time, I organized a day of meditation at the local sporting arena. The open area and offices above the arena were available for community events. It was the first time I had organized an event like this and I had both my sons with me. At the end of the day, we used a small truck to transport all the stock that we had used for the event.

My sister called me unexpectedly and informed me that she was separating from her relationship and needed my help right away to get her belongings out of her house. We decided on the spur of the moment that it was time for us to live together as we had once promised to do, inspired by grandmother Jeanne and her sister Imelda. My nephew was only six months old and my boys were eleven and nine at the time.

We managed to locate a big truck and my brother Alain came and helped us relocate her belongings to my house. The weather changed rather suddenly and a big snowstorm began. We were fortunate that we managed to move all of her possessions inside before the weather worsened.

It was such a blessing for us to all live together. We both shared the bills and we looked after each other's children. We learnt to rely on each other which meant that we could continue to live as independent women whilst sharing parenthood. I continued my university studies at night while Marie-Josée stayed with my sons. I minded her son early in the morning when she left for work with the electrical company, Hydro-Quebec. My sister was one of the first females to work outdoors in what was generally considered a man's job, erecting electrical poles. She is a very intelligent woman who developed into a very determined and motivated woman, excelling in her field. Both of my boys were very impressed and inspired by her work.

On my way to work at CREL, I would take my nephew to daycare. Across the road from the center was an abandoned white house. It was owned by a local bank, Caisse Populaire de Saint Jerome. As the bank couldn't find tenants for the house, it was only used as a warehouse and storage depot for old furniture. The bank lodged planning applications to demolish the house and turn the land into a parking lot. Several local citizens and I wrapped chains around the house and attached ourselves with locks, protesting that it was a historical heritage site and shouldn't be destroyed. Our actions saved the house from being demolished. We referred to it as 'The White House'.

I could see my grandmother becoming frailer with each passing day. She kept saying that she didn't want to be here anymore. Although I was working quite far away, I made sure I had enough time to visit her every night at the nursing home. She kept telling me she didn't want to die until her mother, Clara Bourgeois' memory was acknowledged.

It was during this period that many businesses in Quebec closed down. The Quebec Workers Federation decided that they would only give contracts to businesses that had a union. My manager decided to establish a union at our workplace. I refused to be a part of that union, even though my colleagues signed up because we were a co-operative of workers. I felt it was contrary to my democratic rights to be forced to join a union against my will. I was so stressed about it that I remember having blood in my stool from the stress of that change.

I decided that I couldn't remain in that environment. I was thirty two years old and decided to take early retirement from paid work and start the organizations that I wanted to create. I had saved money from my work and the day care centers and that would support me for a while. I used my time to focus on several endeavors, one being the inauguration of a foundation called the Clara Bourgeois Foundation, in memory of my great grandmother. I also wanted to set up some meetings to unite various religious groups and I also needed to continue developing the Coffret Center. I lived off my retirement savings for three years so that I could set up my organizations.

In 1991 I lodged an application with the Government of Quebec to obtain assistance with the development of the Coffret. They accepted my proposal and I began to receive funding, which also included my salary, from the government for the center. The ball had started rolling and I was thrilled. We worked tirelessly over the next four years to ensure that all the immigration centers within Quebec, including the Coffret in the Laurentians region, were endorsed to receive immigrants and refugees. We started a Regional Council of Immigration where all relevant parties assembled to outline and adopt services to cater for the needs of refugees that were to be accepted into the country. Most of these people had little exposure to or knowledge of the refugee situation and we needed to convince them to accept and welcome the refugees. The first official meeting was in 1992 and we worked with several partners concerned with immigration in our area to prepare the Coffret.

At the same time, I approached two women to help me set up the Clara Bourgeois foundation. I came up with the idea of the foundation at University. I had spent some time with the Local Center of Social Services (CLSC) and saw that there was no organization set up for families, children or women in need. I thought that by establishing this foundation, I could partner with the CLSC and have a place where people from the community could go if they needed assistance. I had discussions with other students and they all agreed that we should name the foundation after my great grandmother.

We approached the bank with a view to using the 'White house' for my foundation but they refused saying they wanted a prestigious organization or a legal service such as a notary or law office to occupy the building. We presented many offers to the bank and arranged for architects, engineers, plumbers and electricians to look at the house so that we had a file of quotes and other information outlining what we wanted to accomplish in the house. We made multiple proposals but they kept finding reasons to refuse our offer. We were three women but they kept referring to us as three little girls. We were insulted.

Every time a tradesman came to that house, I had to go and get the janitor from the bank's administration who had to get dressed, go outside and unlock the door. As he was always annoyed by our interruptions, I suggested that if he gave us the key, we would not have to bother him constantly to unlock the door. He agreed and gave us the key.

With the precious key in our possession, we basically barged into the house and began renovating it. We repaired the furnace to start the heating and plugged in the phone lines etc.

The bank realized what we were doing and they were furious that we had managed to gain access. They came every day to tell us to leave but I told them that we weren't leaving because it was an old abandoned building that nobody was using and it should be used for community service. I told them that we wanted a lease but they kept refusing.

One year later we were still working out of the 'White House' but we still didn't have a lease. We submitted another proposal to the bank's administration board. On the day of their meeting, there was a big snowstorm and many of the bank's board of directors who commuted to work, could not get to work. That meant that only local resident board members were there. They voted on our submission and agreed to support our application because they wanted something productive to be done with the 'White House'.

The next day, we were advised that our submission was successful but that the bank managers and the missing administrators were furious when they found out about it. They hired a lawyer to create a lease, thinking that we would not want to sign it. I told them that they were wasting their time because I would sign whatever lease he presented and I wouldn't even read it. I told them that we were staying in that house.

In 1992, there was an article in the local newspaper about the Clara Bourgeois Foundation and the White house. The title of the article was "The Clara Bourgeois Foundation sets foot in the White House". I immediately took the article to my grandmother Jeanne at the nursing home.

Some days later, I went to visit her as per usual. When I entered her room I immediately noticed that her furniture and belongings were not there and assumed that they had moved her to another room. I was informed by the nurses that she had died earlier that day. There were no cell phones at the time so no-one could notify me; they had to wait until I arrived. I cried uncontrollably for a very long time. I had lost my grandmother, a sister, and a friend.

My grandmother had organized her funeral and covered all the expenses prior to her death so everyone just needed to turn up to the service. It was an extremely sad time for my whole family. I think of her all the time and remember how she waited here on earth until the memory of her mother was recognized in our community.

This period of my life was extremely busy: my divorce, my sister moving in with me, my studies, my organizational commitments and my grandmother's death. There was a lot happening in my life but I managed, mainly because my sister and I were living together and sharing the responsibility of the children.

In 1995 my sister decided to buy her own house and moved out after nearly five years of our living together. My nephew didn't want to leave as he enjoyed our united family unit.

My eldest son, Mathieu was sixteen years old at that stage and he approached me, asking me for my permission to enroll in the army. I refused to give him my consent. I did not want him going away and being killed in a war. He approached me again when he turned eighteen and I again refused to sign any application forms.

My parents kept on going to Mexico. My father's health was deteriorating and he would set off in in a wheelchair and with an oxygen tank. The cold in Canada was not good for him. Once he arrived in the warmth of Mexico, he could walk properly and didn't need the oxygen tank.

In 1995 I received a video cassette from someone in Rwanda showing me footage of what was happening in Africa at the time. I played the footage and was horrified and saddened to see the war zones and entire communities massacred with machetes. I experienced heart palpitations when I thought about the terrible predicament of these African people. I felt helpless and powerless because I couldn't go there and help them.

The unfathomable aggression and cruelty that occurs in war zones in countries around the world brings me to a point where I believe that only through prayer and meditation can we bring a certain consciousness to the people who are so highly insensitive.

As part of my work in establishing the Coffret, we decided to establish an inter-religious committee to bring together representatives from many different religious groups. It was set up as a philosophic forum where we exchanged ideas and tried to develop common values to promote harmony between the different ethnic and cultural communities in our territory.

I went to the Buddhist temple in Verdun, Montreal to request a monk to attend our committee meetings.

I then approached the biggest Orthodox Jewish Community in Boisbriand. They refused many times to join our committee so I tried another approach. I met a man that worked within the Quebec Government with Jewish relations. I requested him to give me the contact details for the Grand Rabbi and he obliged. I contacted the Grand Rabbi and said "Listen, I absolutely have to know who you are and I want my sons to know who you are, and you should introduce your sons to us so that in fifty years' time they won't be killing each other in a war. You didn't come to Quebec to create conflict so we need to ensure that we know each other and can live in peace together."

It worked. He agreed to send a Rabbi who worked as a teacher in Joliette. He came to our meetings and we laughed a lot with him. We even organized a visit to the Jewish community center in Boisbriand and we were made to feel very welcome.

After that outing, we visited the Buddhist Temple, the Hindu Ashram in Val-Morin and the Greek Orthodox nuns of Brownsburg. The nuns were extraordinary. There were about twenty of them and they were all very young, approximately twenty years old.

After I met with the nuns, I was at home one night and at about 11pm I heard a knock at my door. Two of the nuns had brought over some young sisters from Greece who had visa and passport problems. They wanted my help with the paperwork. It was because of those nuns that I became very close to the Greek Orthodox community in Brownsburg, visiting them on many occasions.

I approached a Muslim imam to join our committee and he helped us develop a very objective and positive attitude towards Islam. As he wasn't a fundamentalist or militant, nor perceived by the group as a potential terrorist, he was a very interesting addition to our group and he helped change how we viewed the Islamic people that arrived in our region. Many Muslims who settled in Quebec integrated well into our society.

I approached many different leaders and, in the end, our members comprised of Orthodox Jews, a Buddhist monk, a Muslim imam, Catholic priests and Protestant pastors from local congregations and many more.

Our meetings were extremely productive.

From these relationships, I was also able to organize community gatherings. I decided to hold a presentation at my former high school, the Polyvalent School. I wanted to introduce the 5th grade students to the monk from the temple so that they could learn about the Buddhist way of life.

An elderly monk, Kenji came with two younger monks who would translate for him and they gave a presentation in the school auditorium. Kenji did not speak French and when he arrived in front of the students, he quietly sat down and the children stopped talking immediately. He started speaking about the Dalai Lama and what His Holiness has accomplished through compassion, love, diplomacy and understanding. The students listened to his words attentively and some had tears in their eyes from his beautiful and inspirational stories. They were thoroughly intrigued and asked many questions. The teachers were in disbelief to see their students being so attentive to someone. It was not a common occurrence for their attention to be so centered. For me, Kenji was a man with incredible charisma and an intense aura that captivated people and drew them to listen to his message.

In 1995 I joined the Regional Counsel for the Development of the Laurentians and by 1996, I became a member of its executive council. This enabled me to develop sound relations with our partners in immigration because we met often and made decisions on many different issues.

One day, the monk, Kenji came to my office to see me. He needed help with changing the zoning of a particular area in the Laurentians region. He explained to me that a North American woman from the USA had had a vision to go deep into the woods of North America and find a tree with seven branches. Once she found the tree, it was there that she should establish a temple. She came to the Laurentians region and found the tree with the seven branches but it was in an agricultural area. She approached the local council and they were against the idea of a temple development because they thought it would encourage an influx of Asian immigrants into the area. They were also afraid that there would be busloads of people invading their farming areas.

Kenji asked me to speak to the mayor. I knew them all as they were on the Regional Counsel with me but I wasn't sure if I would be able to influence their opinions. I thought I would at least make an attempt to approach them on the matter. I wrote a letter stating that the construction of a Buddhist temple is a cultural development and that their investment in the region would help develop the area. I told them that it was a place of worship where people came to meditate and that there would not be droves of buses. The mayors approved the development and as a thank you gesture Kenji gave me a mandala.

The Dalai Lama came to visit the monk Kenji at the Montreal temple and then went on to Los Angeles. Kenji was an elderly monk and thought that if he were to die, he could not wish for anyone more special to conduct his funeral service than the Dalai Lama. He phoned the Dalai Lama and requested that his holiness pass by the temple in Montreal on his way back to Nepal. The Dalai Lama agreed and returned. When he arrived he asked for Kenji. The other monks told him that Kenji was meditating and they waited for several hours before going to check on him. When they entered the room they realized that Kenji had induced death through his meditation. The Dalai Lama remained to conduct the funeral service in the Tibetan tradition.

Kenji's ability to master his own life makes me think about the concept of euthanasia. That story touched me deeply as it made me see that in our life we can accomplish greatness through our own beliefs and if we are clear about what we want, we can make anything happen.

From a very young age, thanks to my uncle Jacques and later through Kenji, I understood more clearly why Buddhism is often not classed as a religion but as a philosophy – a state of being which can be achieved by everyone and where Buddha is not considered a God. It is this Buddha-like state of mind that elevates us to a higher state of consciousness. For me, Buddhism gives humans power to take their life in their hands and become what they want to become. It appears contrary to the Catholic Church which does not encourage people to become who they want to become, but rather to become what the church feels they should be. From this reflection, I came to realize that through the understanding of many religions and beliefs, we can grow to be who we want to be and that it is possible to achieve anything and everything.

I believe in reincarnation because I was told at a young age that Christ was the reincarnation of Eli. For me, this was a very real occurrence even though the Catholic Church does not recognize this. I consider myself as Christian in my beliefs as it is Christ's message that remains with me above other doctrines. I have twelve biographies of Christ and a huge collection of artworks of the Last Supper that I have acquired from my travels to Mexico, Italy and various places around the world. I am convinced that one of the twelve apostles is a woman so each of the sculptures and pieces in my collection depicting the Last Supper has a woman in them. I believe that there was a woman present at the time of Jesus's death and resurrection. I also believe that the church was initially organized contrary to the will of Jesus, in that it was formed to give the male gender sole power.

Chapter XIV

The issue of refugees started during the last World War. There were so many refugees in Europe that the United Nations formed various relief organizations. They eventually became the office of the UN High Commissioner for Refugees which was only meant to be a temporary body. The UNHCR was expected to take care of vast numbers of people who couldn't go back to their own countries. After the war in Europe, other wars started in Asia, Africa and South America. Many were caused by decolonization or by the formation of new countries, such as Pakistan's division from India. Due to the increase in wars and the resulting increase in global refugees, the temporary UNHCR became a permanent organization.

In the past when refugees fled to neighboring countries, the police and army had the right to force them back and many were subsequently killed as a result. After various protocols were added throughout the years to the terms of the original laws of the Geneva Convention of 1949, many of these killings stopped. Nowadays, when refugees flee their country, they can lodge an application to the UNHCR. They need to state their reasons for applying, verify their identity and then wait to see if they qualify for refugee status and UN assistance. The status that they are given depends on whether it is safe for them to eventually return to their country. They are given three options:

1. To wait for the war to settle and then return to their country. The difficulty with this option is that their homes and surrounding vicinities have often been totally destroyed or taken over by rebel groups.

2. To apply for residency in the country of refuge. In Europe, this can be very favorable, however in Africa, the country they flee to is often also in the middle of an armed conflict.

3. To wait to be accepted in a new country that is accepting refugees.

In order to comply with UN regulations and process our first refugees there were a multiple formalities to complete. I had to present a submission on behalf of the local authorities and organizations outlining their agreement to accept the refugees, even though we had our own social issues. I needed to provide an exhaustive list of committees and supporting evidence for each criterion to show that we had the means to address our existing social difficulties whilst being able to provide access to a variety of services to help the refugees integrate acceptably into our society.

One part of my job is to ensure that the local community remains in a healthy and harmonious state so that we can continue accepting refugees. The other part involves leading a team of professionals to monitor health and education facilities and deal with related issues to make certain that all is progressing well with the integration of our immigrants.

In Quebec we have eighteen regions and each region has a capital. Saint Jerome is the capital of the Laurentians region. Amongst the regions, Saint Jerome is the only one with a 'Francization' program, a process aimed at keeping French as the primary language of business and commerce and the cultural assimilation required to achieve that goal. There is a similar center to the Coffret in the 18 regions of Quebec. They are all not for profit, non-government organizations.

Within the Laurentians region, we have an average immigration intake of 3.5% of the current population. My studies have indicated that, at no time, should we have more than a 5% intake or else the integration into the community could be jeopardized.

Our first refugees arrived in 1995-96 and were from the former Yugoslavia. They were displaced because of the independence wars in Serbia, Bosnia and Croatia. Many refugees who arrived from Sarajevo had university degrees and due to their former education had a relatively quick migration process, integrated well and found jobs within a short period of time. It was wonderful to welcome them to our country.

The next refugees arrived from Africa in 1996. It was hard for them to open up and discuss what was happening in their countries. It was just too traumatic for them. It was important for us to spend time with some of the African men because in their home countries, men traditionally have authority over women and many have several wives. These customs and beliefs were imbedded and we needed to enlighten them as to our fundamental principles and standards of equality. Some of the wives were exposed to male dominance or domestic violence in Africa. After arriving here and learning about our standards and laws, some wanted to divorce their husbands due to the poor treatment they had received from them in their home country. Not all families were in this situation. Some other families were educated, the husbands were monogamous and lived in harmony with their wife and children, they had strong Christian ethics and prayed for a peaceful world.

A few years ago, I had to speak with one of the fathers who arrived with ten children with another on the way. I explained to him that it would be difficult for him and irresponsible, to keep having children every year when he wasn't in a position to support them. He didn't appreciate a woman broaching these issues with him and I could see that he struggled with my advice. He wouldn't consider a vasectomy. When his pregnant wife went to hospital for a check-up it was discovered that the child had died. He insisted that his wife have a hysterectomy so that he would not be subjected to a vasectomy.

I had to intervene in their family issues on many occasions because he couldn't understand that in our country we prefer to take a softer approach within our family units. He is very strict with his many children and I can see that some of the older children are struggling with his disciplinary ways. In Africa, they had several mothers because their father had multiple wives. It is tough on some of them as they are here without their birth mother. On one occasion, their apartment caught fire and we had to relocate them to another apartment building. It was difficult because other residents in the area were afraid that another fire would occur. It took almost one year to relocate them into a permanent apartment.

Some integrations are more challenging than others but overall, our new arrivals integrate well into our society and we are trying hard to offer help to victims of war. If only we could find a solution to preventing wars and hence stopping the number of refugees from rising.

In 1997, my parents were away in Mexico when my father became terribly ill. They rushed him back to the hospital in Saint Jerome. I went to see him at the hospital and could see that he was in very poor health. It was a very difficult time for my mother, seeing him suffering in this way. On 31st May, the inauguration of the 8-mile long Confederation Bridge, which stretches from New Brunswick to Prince Edward Island, was to take place. My father really wanted to see the bridge before he died but he had not had the chance. I told him that I would organize it. I found a van to hire and planned to take my father, along with his oxygen tanks to view the bridge and opening celebrations. I knew that it would make him very happy to see that bridge. I planned to take him there eventually.

A few months later, in September, I had a very important meeting with the Ministry for Employment and several other delegates. We were seated at a large conference table discussing strategies to address poverty and trying to formulate programs that we hoped to introduce. During the break, I saw a message on my phone from the Saint Jerome hospital to come quickly because my father was in a critical condition and they were not sure how much longer he would live. I almost passed out and fell to the floor, crying uncontrollably. I could not get up because of the shock of hearing the news. A friend at the meeting consoled me and drove me to the hospital. It was mid-morning when I arrived at the hospital. My mother and siblings, except for one brother, who was making his way on a flight, were already there.

We stood around the bed and watched my father as he lay there unconscious. We talked to him and thanked him for everything that he had done for us. We stood around his bed for several hours and at noon, my mother took my siblings to have some lunch. I decided to remain with my father.

I kept talking to him, telling him how grateful we were to him and how it was a relief that he was leaving in peace. Suddenly, I saw his ring finger turn blue. I quickly tried to take the ring off his finger but as I was trying, he died. I called the family back and twenty minutes later my other brother finally arrived from the airport. He was in despair that he hadn't made it in time to say goodbye. My mother had been looking after my father whilst he was in intensive care and she knew how much he was suffering. He had said that he wanted to die at 64, and now he was 67. He knew that it was his time to pass. Even though I didn't manage to drive my father across the bridge that he loved so much, we are all convinced that he passed over that bridge before leaving this world for the next.

I left the hospital and decided to go for a walk in the park near my home. My father came to me whilst I was walking and said, "Don't worry, there's balance, there's justice, everything's perfect. Don't worry." It was my last conversation with him.

Over the next few days my mother and I organized the funeral service which was held at the church in Saint Antoine. The casket was open for viewing beforehand at the funeral home. My father was involved in politics and had many friends and contacts in the whole region. Many people loved and appreciated him and there was a big crowd at his funeral. It was such a sad time for our family.

I inherited many wonderful traits from both my parents such as their sociability, organizational skills, their capacity to motivate people and to share their beliefs with others. I developed their strength and courage to face people and to tell them directly what they need to do to deal with their issues and responsibilities. My mother had a great sense of compassion towards others and an unending willingness to help people. Even today, she is a mediator at the nursing home, defending others and helping them. My father had a great sense of humor and I know I inherited this trait from him. He could make people laugh through terrible situations whilst trying to find solutions to their issues. Even though my father has passed, I know that he will always remain with me.

My father

Mathieu was 21 years old by now and did not need my authority to join the army. Staying true to his convictions from three years of age, on the day of his 21st birthday he told me that he had joined the army and was leaving for Saint Jean du Richelieu. My other son, Jérémé had finished secondary school and left for Montreal to complete further studies. I had a big house with no children in it. I decided that a couple of dogs at the house would be nice company.

Meanwhile, the new bishop who arrived in Saint Jerome made it known that he did not approve of the inter-religious committee. He approached me saying that the Coffret had no authority to lead this type of council. He contacted all the members and told them to stop coming to the meetings. Although we organized a few activities after his intervention, the council wound up soon afterwards. We were proud of our achievements during the eight years that we were active.

It was winter time and Christmas was fast approaching. My mother kept travelling to Mexico each winter on her own and I decided to have a Christmas celebration for the French tutors of the Coffret that year. One of the tutors told me that he would invite a young Chinese girl who had recently arrived from China. He was teaching her French at the local school. When I met her, I remember thinking how cute she looked, even though she looked like a little boy. It was immensely enjoyable for us all to get together for the Christmas celebration and I could see how much the staff appreciated the gesture.

It snowed heavily this particular winter and, as usual, I enjoyed doing lots outside. I went dog-sledding with my dogs one day and managed to catch my fingers in the rope. My fingers turned blue and I was in a lot of pain. I had dinner with my friend Francois that evening and had a few drinks to try and numb the pain. As I couldn't continue drinking I left early to get a good night's sleep.

That night, my father appeared in my dreams. It hadn't been long since his passing so it was comforting to see him in my dreams. I asked him what he was doing here.
He said, "Don't tell anybody, I'm here just for you, I've arranged everything and everything will be okay." I had no idea what he was referring to.

The next morning, a Sunday, Francois called to check on my fingers. They were still painful but getting better. He told me that he had just received a strange phone call from his friend asking if he knew of anyone who could find a home for a young Chinese girl. As there is a twelve hour time difference between Canada and China, I wondered if this matter of the young Chinese girl had arisen at the same time as my father appeared in my dream.

Francois told me that her name was Jin but she preferred to be called Jennifer so as to sound more American. I then realized that it was the same Chinese girl that I had met at the Christmas party. I told Francois that I would gladly welcome her into my home. I like to call her Jin.

Jin's parents lived in China where her father worked for a big Canadian company. One of his employment benefits was that the company would pay for the entire cost of private tuition if his child studied in Canada. As Jin's godfather was living in Sainte Therese, Quebec, her father contacted him for assistance. They decided it was best that the father rent an apartment in Montreal so that Jin would have the opportunity to get a better education at a superior school. Her mother couldn't come with her because she couldn't get a visa to stay here for such a long time. Her father accompanied her to Montreal and, with the help of her godfather, arranged for her to attend a school in Saint Jerome and live in the care of a foster family.

Jin wasn't aware that her father would go back to China and leave her on her own in Canada. She was in a state of complete shock and felt lost and confused, especially as she didn't speak French. There were three other children living at the foster home and it was difficult for all. Jin fell into a state of depression. She stopped eating and cried all the time. As her French tutor was working for me at the Coffret, I had been told how distressed she was and how difficult it was for her emotionally. The school decided that they needed to change her foster family as her current situation was becoming detrimental to her health.

I arranged to take her in and I met with Jin and her godfather at a Saint Hubert restaurant. She realized immediately that we had met at the Christmas party. I took her home and showed her her new room. She stayed in her room for a very long time and didn't want to come out. She was only eleven years old.

I called both of my sons and told them that they had a new sister. They came to the house for dinner that night to meet her. The dinner went really well and she received a warm welcome into our family. She now says that she has two brothers.
Although the boys were much older than Jin at the time, today it is as if they are the same age.

Jin continued to adjust to the significant changes in her day-to-day routines as life here in Quebec was very different to what she had known previously. She explained how, in China, her walk to school took her alongside the canals. There she saw dead baby girls lying in the canals. As parents were only allowed to have one child, unwanted baby girls were dumped in the waterways so that parents could have another chance at a baby boy in order to pass on the family name. Some of the babies were still alive and screaming but she knew she wasn't allowed to pick them up. This information totally shocked me. I couldn't believe that innocent babies were discarded in this manner and deprived of their right to life.

Some immigrants, when they arrive in our country, don't have the insight to understand the basic concepts of life with which we have been raised. They are required to begin a journey of ongoing adjustment and need to re-program their thoughts on the right to life, equity, freedom, ethics, human dignity and many other values. We are born into our first world societal concepts but they are not. There is often no comparison between our reference points and theirs.

When my dogs had a litter Jin, who had never had a dog before, asked if she could keep one and named him Picasso. The dog kept her company and became her baby and her brother. Her father kept saying that he had a daughter and son, Picasso, in Canada. It was funny to hear this. One day, Jin told me that she wanted to become a French Canadian, a Quebecoise.

Not long after she moved in with us, I received four loads of wood logs for the fire. We had to hurry and pile up the logs before the snow and ice penetrated the wood. There were a few of us in a line stacking the logs. She asked if she could help so we let her take a place in the log chain. We were all thoroughly exhausted afterwards.

The next morning I received a call from her school telling me to come quickly as Jin could not move. They said it was as if she were paralyzed. The school may have thought that I was mistreating her by making her do such heavy work as piling up logs. The episode became somewhat amusing as I tried to explain to the school principal that it was Jin's idea to help so she could show that she was tough enough to be involved in the task. I still laugh about that episode.

In early 1998, we received refugees from Colombia, a country which has experienced wars and conflict for over 60 years. Four million Colombians took refuge in neighboring Ecuador, a small country that couldn't accommodate such an influx of people. Ecuador accepted the refugees on a temporary basis on condition that they were relocated. Many Colombians were accepted by countries in

Europe, the USA and Canada. Saint Jerome has a large population of more than 650 Colombians.

As many Colombians were not prepared to learn French it made it hard for us to help assimilate them into the system. I knew that I had to do something to address this issue. If people are accepted as immigrants, they must be willing to fit into our established society or else it will create problems socially within our own communities. We cannot allow that to occur because it will prevent us from helping people who are willing to embrace all aspects of their new lives.

In June 1988, we received our first refugees from Kosovo. Their arrival presented us with a different situation. Usually, refugees who flee their country settle in a refugee camp for a period of time before being relocated to the next country. This allows them some time to accept their circumstances and for any internal tensions to subside a little. In the case of Kosovo, in the midst of deep conflict with Serbia, we needed to send a plane from Canada to rescue some people who were trapped on a mountain and at risk of losing their lives. With them arrived others who had been temporarily sheltered in Macedonia for a short time. We had not experienced that level of urgency before. They were all flown out of the war zone as quickly as possible and the government didn't even have time to prepare their identity papers. When they arrived they were sent to the military base in Kingston, near Toronto. They remained there until we had time to prepare their papers and decide to which area they would be sent.

I remember receiving an urgent fax containing a list of names of people from Kosovo who were coming to Saint Jerome. It was as if the names fell out of the sky and into our office. There were ninety-two people on the list but only four last names. We assumed that they must be big family groups like our clans. We had no idea who was part of each family so that we could arrange accommodation and other services. I decided to go to Kingston to meet with them. Mathieu was back from Bosnia at the time so he accompanied me to the military base.

I walked into the Quebec Immigration Office that was set up in a Winnebago van and told them why I was there. They directed me to the mess to meet with the new arrivals. There were 3000 people in there. I walked in and a little ten year old girl, whom I had never met before, ran into my arms, hugged me and it was like she said "Where were you?" I greeted her warmly and her family came straight over to find about the woman who had embraced their daughter. It was a moment that I'll never forget and one of many where I meet people that I feel I have known my entire life or met in another lifetime due to the instant connection and understanding. Regardless of age or whether we speak the same language, it is a connection that comes from having known each other. That little girl and her entire family were on the list to Saint Jerome so we sat with them to work out who was who. There were 35 people in the one family. A week later, they arrived in Saint Jerome and we helped them settle in.

Some of the families did not want to live close to each other as a big group and they specifically requested to live in separate areas. That made it easier for us because it was difficult to find apartments that housed twelve people. One of the families that I dealt with was absolutely amazing. I would say they were probably the best-integrated family that we have had: a big family but very close and loving towards each other and others.

Many more families from Kosovo arrived in our region. Our staff accompanied them to their apartments, took them shopping and showed them the ropes. Some of the men were aggressive towards my staff and two of my employees resigned because they could not handle dealing with them. This meant that I had to take some of them shopping myself. At the Center we are allocated a certain amount of funding for each refugee and a list of what we must purchase for them. I need to strictly comply with these conditions in order to receive future funding. I took one of the men to the shops and asked him to pick a dress and a pair of pants for his elderly mother. He indicated that he wanted to pick dresses only. I told him that I could only purchase what was authorized. He became very annoyed and started yelling at me. I could not do anything about it and he could not understand. He spat in my face – an act which hurt and upset me greatly.

His family was experiencing another traumatic upheaval in their lives and could not cope with living here in Canada. They eventually decided to go back to Kosovo. This happened at times because of the ongoing terrors that these people had experienced and the sudden cultural change in their lives. We need to accept that we must allow them a period of transition. With sound integration policies and practices, and with the support and compassion of the entire community, we can help these displaced families to start a new life.

At the end of 1998, Jin's parents decided to come and join us for Christmas. They arrived in New York on Christmas Eve and called to say that they had trouble renting a car upon arrival in Montreal. They asked if I could find a car for them in Saint Jerome. It was almost impossible to find a car on the 24th December but I managed to find one in Lafontaine, Saint Jerome. The car needed to be picked up by 5pm, but as they were not going to make it by then, I explained to the owner that we could only collect it when they arrived that evening.

They caught a taxi to my home in Saint Antoine and finally arrived at 11pm. I was at home with Jin waiting for them. When Jin's mother came to the door, I soon realized she didn't speak English or French. There was no time for introductions and it seemed as if I was being evicted from my own house. Jin's mother went inside and I left with her father to get the car. I had to quickly familiarize myself with their cultural ways. It took a little while to understand each other's customs.

In China Jin's mother had been given a three-week visa for Canada but when she arrived the authorities stamped her passport for six months. She was so happy that she could stay longer than expected. Three weeks later, we received a call from the Chinese authorities saying that she had to get back to China immediately because she had overstayed her three-week visa. She became very anxious, quickly gathered her belongings and, before she left, I invited the family to a local Asian restaurant for a farewell dinner. I could tell she was extremely stressed and Jin translated her concerns to me.

Jin explained that when her mother returned to China she would have to work one year without a salary for overstaying her visa as this was considered as an illegal act. I told her that they didn't have the right to do that. Jin told me that the word 'Right' does not exist in Chinese bureaucracy. It was a difficult notion to fathom. Her mother wanted to live as a Buddhist but in China she could not do so freely and openly. Their country's fundamental concepts were so different to ours. I was appalled at the situation facing her and, with concern in our hearts, we said our goodbyes. Luckily for Jin's mother, her husband lodged paperwork through his company and within two years she was able to come to Canada as a permanent resident. We lived together for one year in my house until they bought a house in Saint Jerome.

When Jin's mother arrived back in Canada, I took her to the Buddhist temple in Arundel on many occasions. She came across the small library that was full of books. It was in a complete mess as there were no volunteers to take care of the books which were scattered everywhere. She began to cry seeing these sacred books on the ground and she immediately started to pick them up. She decided to become a volunteer worker at the temple.

In 2000, I received many complaints from schools about the children from Kosovo. It was clear that the integration was problematic. We decided to have a day camp with these children.

I approached a professional organization called RIVO who worked with victims of organized violence in Montreal. They helped us develop a strategic scenario to allow the children to work through the cycle of violence that they had experienced in their homeland. There were three stages:

1. Personalize their pre-war identity.
2. Pass through the conflict.
3. Project them into the future.

At that time there was no adequate financing coming into the Center so I applied to receive my work insurance funds to be able to support myself. I decided to run the day camps throughout the summer period from my home.

We reached the first objective by doing book research in my home library. We made photocopies of photos and images and exhibited each picture showing their pre-war identities. We dressed them in their national costumes and presented a show for their parents and our partner organizations.

The second objective required them to draw their former homes on a piece of cardboard. They had a difficult time drawing their houses from memory because they were emotional.

We had a lot of space in my home so they spread out and began to draw big houses. They also drew their families, including their grandparents and extended families, similar to our clans. They sketched farm animals and gardens and all their houses were very similar. They all appeared to be enormous free-standing houses and self sufficient properties.

There were twelve children and the youngest one drew flames leaping from the house. He also drew his grandfather, dead on the floor. Another child drew cadavers in the woods behind the house. A little girl turned to me and said, "Line, the policemen were not very nice to us". I started to reply to her with, "Well, it's not nice but you know…" Before I could finish my sentence, another child with a trembling voice said, "Line, they really were not nice to us".

I realized then that these children had been directly involved in the conflict and that it was all going to come out. I didn't feel I could handle the situation alone. As a delay tactic, I told them that we should prepare lunch. We started cutting the carrots but they couldn't stop. The next little girl said, "Line, the policemen were very, very mean".

I knew that I had to stop everything and listen to them. I sat down and told them that we could talk about what happened. It was terrible. The events they described to me were some of the most horrific that I had ever heard. They saw the Serbian police and army attacking people and committing unbelievable atrocities. They saw women being nailed to doors, in the way that Jesus was nailed to the cross, and then being sexually assaulted, violently and repeatedly. They saw pregnant women who had been cut open with their insides extracted. They saw babies being cut into pieces. They witnessed such horrendous scenes that no child, or adult for that matter, should ever witness.

They continued screaming out their horrific experiences and then they cried, and cried and cried until they got it all out. Then one of the girls, Ariana said "But here, there are probably some sad children too. Maybe we could help them". Another one said, "Maybe we can go to visit some sick children at the hospital".

Finally, they passed through the reliving of the conflict and described their aspirations for the future. The children changed after that camp and behaved much better at school. As for me, I went to therapy for three years after that day to deal with the disclosures of that session.

In September 2001, municipal election campaigns were underway. The mayor of St Jerome had somehow amalgamated Saint Antoine, Lafontaine and Bellefeuille with Saint Jerome. Although this change had been approved by the minister, I couldn't believe this was done without anyone knowing anything about it. I felt it was an insult to democracy.

I went to see the mayor and told him that I wished to be part of his election party. I explained to him that I wanted to ensure that the forward planning and needs of the towns that were forced to amalgamate were met and that the same services that they had previously experienced would still be available to them.

He declined my request. I told him that if I couldn't be on his team, I would be on the opposing team which consisted of new delegates awaiting the next election. At the time, the Mayor of Saint Antoine became the leader of this opposing political party due to the circumstances surrounding the fusion. Around the 8th September he had a cardiac arrest and was told to resign for health reasons. We needed to find a new leader so we scheduled a meeting for the night of 11th September.

I was Vice President of the Regional Council of Development and I needed to hold a meeting with all the partners in the North Laurentians region so that we could discuss the issues concerning the changes to our area. I chaired this meeting.

All who attended were able to present submissions requesting amendments to policies in order to help develop their businesses. At one point, we looked outside the window and saw a commotion. Someone opened the door and yelled, "Come quick. The USA is being attacked".

The hotel placed a big TV in the hall and we sat in disbelief watching the second tower crumble down. I kept thinking about my son, how he was deployed in Bosnia and if this incident started a war, my son would be involved in the fighting. I fell apart inside and thought, "Oh my God. What is happening in the world?"

I was convinced that it was the beginning of World War III. Everyone was so emotional and shocked. I wanted to stop the meeting but as we had people who had travelled from other regions to attend the meeting, we had to proceed.

A participant commented that "When people find themselves in situations where they are not respected, things like New York happen". I blew a fuse at his comment telling him that he was completely off track and it was unrealistic to compare his local situation at the time to the problem with Islam or New York. I postponed the meeting at that point and called for an emergency meeting with all the authorities about the attack on the World Trade Center.

As the authorities came together, I wanted to make sure that we were prepared for the possibility that we may have an influx of people fleeing the USA and other travelers avoiding the USA due to the terrorists attacks in New York. Mirabel airport authorities made space for flights that were diverted from New York to Mirabel. The Association of Tourism for the Laurentides was aware that we needed to accommodate many unexpected arrivals and every available hotel room and other lodging was prepared throughout the region.

Once this matter was under control, I raced to the night meeting to determine who would run for mayor. All the municipal councilors from every district introduced themselves and, one by one, found a good reason as to why they couldn't run for mayor of the new Saint Jerome. One of the councilors looked at me and said, "Line, you are the only one who can run for Mayor".

I kept thinking about my son away at war and the possibility of a third world war and decided that this could be my way of having a say in what happens in the future. I agreed to become a candidate for mayor. The whole election campaign lasted for two months and I was very committed to the cause. I was winning the campaign until the last votes from Lafontaine were counted, the area where the incumbent mayor had loyal supporters. He managed to win the election by 1000 votes.

As the mayor was angry with me for running against him, in order to punish me, he bought the White House from the bank and evicted us from the house. We had twelve organizations operating out of that building and we all had to go. I couldn't believe his actions. I took all the fittings and started up again in my home. We put a sign on my house and re-named it the "White House".

After September 11, 2001, the Canadian Army aligned with the USA army and entered Afghanistan. This put an end to the soldiers known as Blue Helmets. Soldiers who wore a blue helmet, or blue beret, are part of the UN Peacekeeping Force. They do not engage in any combat but are there to help repair the country and assist civilians. My son wore a blue helmet and when in Bosnia he undertook activities such as building schools and repairing bridges damaged during the war. The goal in Afghanistan was to invade and attack so Blue Helmet army members were instructed to remove their blue helmets and begin offensive training. Mathieu stood up in the middle of a class and left the room. He was arrested and told to go back to training and sit down. He told his seniors that he could not go out and fight. They explained the only way out was to obtain a medical certificate from a doctor stating that, for psychological reasons, he was not able to take part in active combat. He saw a doctor and organized the certificate. At the same time, his girlfriend in Canada was pregnant and he was able to leave the army and come home.

In 2002, I organized a visit to an abandoned church in Saint Lucien that was recently purchased by a group of doctors who wanted to build a medical clinic. The Liberals were now in power and they didn't allow the development to proceed. The doctors agreed to sell it to me and I gave them a $5000 deposit. The mayor found out about the deposit and immediately changed the zoning. An article appeared in the local newspaper titled, *'The town of Saint Jerome changes zoning to stop the Clara Bourgeois Foundation from moving into the Saint Lucien Church'*.

I was appalled at this behavior. I had recently had refugees move into the area and I told them that they were coming into an area of peace. There was a war being waged in Saint Jerome. I asked my cousin who knew the mayor to convince him to speak with me so that we could try to resolve our differences.

We met at a restaurant in front of the Saint Lucien Church. I got there first and went to the bathroom to wash my hands. I looked in the mirror and had a melt-down at that point and started yelling at myself, "It's unreal. You are not going to go down on your knees for him again. He will win. You are not going to ask for pity. Who's he? What's so special about that unconscious man who runs the show? You won't kneel down before him".

I was in the bathroom for twenty minutes in a terrible state until a little voice from my heart, came into my head and said, "No Line, it's not for you that you're doing this, it's for the sake of the refugees". I said, "Yes, it's for others, for refugees who don't even have a country". I regained my self-control.

I walked out calmly and tried speaking about many issues but he didn't want to hear anything. He said that I wasn't going to continue my work in Saint Jerome and he didn't need me there. He basically did not want me to exist in his area. I said goodbye and left the meeting.

I had already lost the $5000 deposit because of him. That was a lot of money for us when we didn't have a lot to start with and I now had to find another premises.

I went to see the parish priest at the Cathedral who was a distant cousin of my maternal great-grandfather.

The first thing he told me when I arrived is, "Do you want Sainte Marcelle Church?"
I said, "Of course I want the church". I hadn't told him why I had come to see him so I was quite taken aback.

He held a meeting that night at the church and announced to all the attendees that the church was closing and that it would be demolished. I saw people crying from the shock of the announcement.

Every church in the area is administrated by a counsel called a FABRIQUE. I contacted the members, offering them a solution to which they agreed. I attended a meeting with the FABRIQUE two days later proposing that we move our organization to Sainte Marcelle Church. They called me an angel, saying that I was an answer to their prayers, but I told them that they were an answer to mine.

It was of mutual benefit to both parties and the FABRIQUE agreed to sell the church to us for one dollar. I agreed that Sunday services would continue as always and that we would organize additional activities.

It was spring at the time and the Bishop of the diocese was away in Rome for a couple of months. I told the parish priest that we were moving in but he said that we could not do that until the Bishop returned and approved the sale. The Bishop had the final word.
I told the parish priest that the Bishop had just closed down Saint Adolphe D' Howard and we cannot keep on closing down churches or else they will all become abandoned like the church in Saint Lucien.

The Bishops had a lot of authority in the Laurentians region at that time. It had been that way for many years. They also work closely with the church ministers. I was unable to persuade the parish priest who decided that they would close the church on 1st July, which also meant that the electricity, water and gas supplies would be disconnected. I knew that to re-open the church and reconnect all the utilities would cost up to $50,000. I kept annoying the parish priest with my many calls every day. On the day before the closure, I called him again telling him that closing the church was a crime against humanity. He finally agreed and told me he would sign the lease over to us and allow us to rent it until the Bishop returned.

We loaded all our furniture and office equipment from the Saint Lucien church into a big truck, moved into the Sainte Marcelle church, connected phone lines and installed ourselves. When the Bishop returned, he was not happy with the decision and wanted us out. I explained to him that we were there to respond to the needs of the community and by being in the church, we were also serving the Lord. We decided to name the building Meridien 74.

The Bishop was so irate that he spoke via a middle-man in the room. The message was that I was to be out by the morning. I told him that we were not moving tomorrow, or the day after that because the church needs to service the community and it is the community that has a need to stay in this church. We stayed on in our blessed building and many people kept trying to force us out.

In the spring of 2003 I decided to do an internship at the Sant' Egidio Community in Rome. I had learned that they took over empty buildings and turned them into places for the needy. The Vatican administers all religious buildings in Rome and when a church or convent closes down, they give it to the Sant' Egidio community. I completed the internship to learn how to manage a church and community building.

After that internship, I came back to Saint Jerome and demonstrated how the transformation of churches can work well in the community. I convinced the FABRIQUE administration that it is the best thing to do. It took one year for us to be in a position to buy our church, which we did in 2004, and finally the Bishop understood what we were trying to achieve. During that time, the community using the church grew and he could see that the church was more alive than ever before. Even now, there are 1500 people that pass through those church doors every week.

Once we were settled in the church, I went on another internship with the Governor General of Canada to witness the method of training of Canada's future leaders. I wanted confirmation that we had enough young potential leaders who knew each other well and would be able to work together successfully.

Chapter XV

Around this time, I received devastating news that my friend Lizanne had died. She developed Crohn's disease and died from it. It is always sad to hear of friends passing because we reflect back over the wonderful experiences that we shared during our lifetimes. Lizanne and I kept in touch over the years. She had a daughter and we tried to remain in contact after Lizanne's death but every time she saw us, it was hard for her emotionally and she gradually distanced herself from us.

In the winter of 2004, I decided to accompany my mother to Mexico. It was a last minute decision and I remember being there with her at the time when the tsunami hit in southern Asia. I remember my intense sadness at hearing of all the deaths. I returned to the Coffret as soon as I came back and my colleagues told me that the Bishop urgently wanted to see me whilst I was away. I had to find strength and kept saying to myself, "I'm not scared of the Pope, so I can't be scared of the Bishop".

I went to see him and he said to me, "Line, we have to organize a memorial service for all the children who died in the tsunami. You're the only one who can do it". I was so surprised that, after all our differences, he finally recognized the worth in what I did and also that he felt that only I could be trusted to arrange certain matters. From that point on we had a very good relationship.

Towards the end of autumn 2005, my brother Michel died from

complications with his illness. He knew that he could die at any time because of the hepatitis he had contracted but he didn't expect it would be at the age of 50. It was terrible. I was in complete shock and disbelief and his wife and two children were distraught. I kept thinking that I was so busy looking after the community that I neglected to look after my own brother. I fell into a deep state of sadness from which I couldn't extract myself. I was living with Jin and her mother during that time and even though I had company around me, I couldn't escape the terrible feeling of extreme loss.

We were raised Catholics but my brother didn't want a funeral service in the church. He just wanted his body to be exposed for viewing at the funeral home and to then be cremated. Jin, her mother and I took candles to place near my brother's body. The funeral home did not allow the candles, telling us that fires of any kind were not allowed within the home. None of us could understand what society had come to when, in a place of mourning, we were not allowed to light candles. It was the first time that we didn't hold a church funeral service for a member of our family so we felt that we needed to do something in his honor.

My youngest son invited family and close friends to my house. We bought some alcohol at the local SAQ, sat around and held a wake for my brother. It was not a tradition that we were used to but, at the time, it was the only way that we thought we could get over the shock of his death.

We were all close with Michel's wife but after his death, she moved further north to Saint Lin with her youngest son so I don't get to see them as much anymore. She doesn't drive so it is difficult for her to get to Saint Jerome. The eldest son was already living near me and he stayed in the area. I used to babysit him when he was young and we still have a very close relationship.

Although the extreme sadness I felt after Michel's death remained with me, I was fully aware that I had a lot of responsibilities. I had numerous employees and I was involved in many organizations and committees. It became difficult for me to make decisions because I kept on questioning why I had not taken greater care of my brother. I told myself that I had made a bad decision and it was haunting me. I needed to get away so that I could re-group and re-center myself but I wasn't sure where to go. Initially I thought of going to Israel but I didn't know anybody there. I then met a friend, Helene who told me that she was going to Abu Dhabi for her exposition. I took this as a sign and decided that it would be a good place to go so that I could gain a greater understanding of the Muslim faith and observe how Middle Eastern people live. I told my friend that I would go with her.

As soon as I made the decision I felt my energy return because I believed that this experience would get me out of my depressed state. I received a call that same day from the sister of one of Michel's friends who called to offer her condolences. I spoke with her and told her that I was going to Abu Dhabi. She told me that her brother was an airline pilot for Emirates and that he lived in nearby Dubai in a pilots' residence. He organized to send me his keys in the mail so that I could stay there for the month as he would be away. I couldn't believe my good fortune. It was a blessing.

I began organizing my trip. This would be a time to recharge myself so that I could face upcoming challenges and accept the ones that I had recently encountered.

In the interim, I put a team together and organized a local carnival in Saint Jerome. Many new immigrants and refugees from warmer climates stayed in their homes the entire winter period as it was just too cold for them to go outside. It didn't make sense to me so I thought a carnival would be a great way to encourage them out of their homes. We planned different kinds of events such as a dog sleigh race. We scheduled the carnival for 10th February, which was also my birthday. We held a team meeting and agreed that it would be a good idea to bring back on old local tradition, that of appointing a Carnival Queen. We organized a ball and asked candidates to dress in gowns representing their native countries. Someone would be crowned Carnival Queen at the event. We decorated the ballroom, laid a red carpet and 250 people attended. My daughter Jin represented China. Each girl had to make a short presentation and at the end of the night everyone voted for their favorite. I wasn't allowed to vote as I was one of the organizers. After the votes were counted and the result announced, we were elated as it was Jin who was crowned Carnival Queen.

It was a great evening and at the end of the night, Jin's mother drove me to the airport with my suitcases and deposited me there at about 2am. A big snowstorm had started and my flight was cancelled. I had to wait many hours until my flight to New York and once there, we could not depart for Dubai because of the weather. I was stuck in the New York airport terminal for about 36 hours. I was the only white woman travelling on her own surrounded by many Arabs and Jews that were flying on Emirates which, at the time, was the most direct service to the Middle East. I was extremely tired and needed to sleep. I went to the bathroom and dozed a little whilst clinging on to my suitcases. I looked for another option. There was a mosque, a synagogue and a small chapel inside the terminal and they were full except for the small chapel. I took my luggage into the chapel and made a little nest, like a homeless person, and fell asleep. I awoke suddenly to the sound of a loud noise. It was the janitor locking the chapel. I raced to tell him that I was inside and he let me out after telling me that I wasn't allowed to sleep in the chapel.

I thanked God for getting me out of the chapel because a few hours later our plane was ready to depart for Dubai.

I travelled alone as my friend Helene was meeting me in Abu Dhabi. When I arrived in Dubai, it was late at night. I didn't speak Arabic and all I had was a map that I drawn of the location of the house. I took out the map and approached a taxi driver to take me to the house. He didn't want to take me because no one wants to transport a woman who is on her own. I could see that they were puzzled as to why I wasn't accompanied by a brother, father or husband. I kept arguing and pleading with them to take me to the house and after many hours of negotiation, an older man agreed to take me. He looked at my map but couldn't make sense of it so he asked others for help in working out the area where the house was located.

When I arrived I was blown away. It wasn't a house, it was a castle. After going inside and settling in I kept on thinking how beautiful it was.

In the early hours of the morning, whilst still dark, I could hear shouts of 'Haaallllaaaahhhhh" and I awoke thinking that there were spirits in the house. I have had many experiences with spirits in my home over the last thirty years. I searched the house for the source of the noise but it had stopped and I couldn't find anything. When I went for a walk later that morning, I discovered that there was a big mosque next door to the 'castle'. The noise that I had heard was the muezzin calling the faithful to the first prayer session of the day. That was the start of my stay in Dubai. It was all so amazing.

On one of the days, Helene and I rented a car to get to Nizwa, the former capital of Oman in the 6th and 7th centuries. Some heavy rain had forced the closure of certain routes. We got lost whilst driving there but managed to find some magnificent ruins that nobody could date. We needed to find the road back so we conceived a short cut through the desert. As soon as we entered the sand dunes, our car got stuck. It reminded me of watching amateur drivers getting stuck in the snow in Quebec.

Suddenly, two gigantic 4 x 4 jeeps arrived with eight young Omani men on board. We didn't speak Arabic but the leader of the group made us believe that he could get us out. He asked us for the keys and, with much hesitation even knowing that I had no choice, I gave him the car keys. Within two to three seconds he had the car out but he didn't want to give us back our car. All the other guys were laughing and my blood pressure was rising.

I screamed to Helene to get into the passenger side of the car. I grabbed the guy and pulled him out of the car, quickly jumped in and did a U-turn in a cloud of sand. I started driving at maximum speed towards the village. The guys jumped in their cars and followed us. We raced through the village and got onto the national highway and travelled for a few kilometers before I felt it was safe enough to stop on the side of the road.

Our hearts were still racing but we took a deep breath and laughed out aloud about our adventure. I believe that the courage I mustered to drag that young Omani man out of my car came from my experience with the refugees from Kosovo. I had to find a way to detach myself from the reality of the situation and do something beyond my natural capabilities and level of tolerance in order to display the authority and strength that I didn't know I was capable of.

Line at the ruins in Oman

My overall experience in Dubai was wonderful. I had no direct previous experiences of the Islamic culture. Many women wore veils and the men dressed differently to what I was used to but I found myself again in that country. I came back to Quebec healed from my mourning and in a strong state of mind to move forward.

The following winter, when my mother was around 76 years of age, she wanted to go to Mexico but I knew she was getting to an age which made it difficult for her to manage all her luggage for the extended stay. I travelled with her a few times to settle her into the apartment but I couldn't always go with her. I had just moved the Coffret to a new location at the church and I was overwhelmed with work. I had many issues with the other organizations that were set up in the same church building and faced some challenging issues.

I kept hearing my deceased father's voice saying that I had to take my mother to Mexico but I didn't feel that I could leave. I awoke one morning and my father's passport was sitting on the kitchen table. I had never seen it there before so I laughed and said out loud, "Okay, okay, I'll do it".

That same day there was a conflict between two organizations that resided in the church. I was up in the bell tower of the church, which was my office at the time, and was heading downstairs as a manager from one of the organizations was walking upstairs towards me. I could see that he was very angry. I knew that he was a violent man and he started yelling at me. I thought to myself, "Oh, thank God I am going to Mexico. It will do me good and it has been a long time since I was in Pie de la Cuesta."

He continued yelling and I kept on day-dreaming about my trip. He said, "Do you understand?" and I said, "Yes, of course", but I hadn't listened to a word of what he had said.

That evening, I collected my mother and without her realizing, I also had my suitcase in the car. I got to the airline counter and asked if there was an available seat on the plane but was told that the flight was completely full. My mother said, "What are you doing?" I told her that I was accompanying her to Mexico.

I asked the counter attendant if I could speak with her boss so that he could personally tell me the plane was full. Begrudgingly, she brought the manager over and I convinced him to find me a seat on the plane. I flew to Mexico with my mother and she was extremely happy because she had several big suitcases that she could not manage on her own.

When we arrived at the apartment, we had to clean it thoroughly and unpack all her boxes as if she were moving in again. This happened every year.

The next morning I took her to Pie de la Cuesta and we saw twelve beautiful dolphins on the beach putting on a show for us. I took this to be a sign from my father, thanking me for taking my mother to Mexico.

As we headed back, I saw a sign about a new archaeological site that had just opened outside Acapulco. I love these sites so I decided to go the next day. My mum didn't want me to go, telling me that I didn't speak Spanish and that it was dangerous for me to go alone.

I got up early and asked the hotel staff where to catch the bus. The bus station was full of local Mexicans. I went to get on the first bus and the driver looked at me and said "No, no, no".

He closed the door and drove off. I waited twenty minutes for the next bus. I saw some people from Quebec getting on the bus and so I thought I would be able to get on this bus but the driver again said "No, no, no". He also closed the door and drove off.

I waited for the third bus and the same thing happened again. I couldn't understand why I couldn't get on a bus. I abandoned my mission and walked back to the hotel. It was quite a long distance so I stopped along the way, visiting local museums. I got home at the end of the day and my mum was so relieved to see me and said "Oh, Oh you're back. Thank God."

I asked "Why?"

She replied, "After you left, I told some people that you had gone to the archaeological site. They all told me that tourists had been kidnapped there and that it was extremely dangerous to go there alone. I prayed to your father to stop you from going".

I replied, "He sure did. I was pushed off three buses".

I chuckled at how my father still stays close to me, even in his spirit form, and helps me with everything I do. Many times his old friends have come to see me over the years and have said things like, "You wouldn't by chance need help with this would you?" It would be exactly what I needed help with and I know it was my father sending his friends to help me.

My mother in her youth

In 2007 I completed some studies at the University (attached to the UN) in Strasbourg, France. The campus was located on the banks of the river that runs through the town. In one session about the United Nations there were fifty of us from all over the world. We were researching how refugees live in some parts of the world. What we learnt was soul destroying. During the break we went outside and sat on a small hill. Everyone was silent. Many of us cried and later had to try and raise our spirits. We were looking out over a valley and I remember, it was at that moment, in the company of this group of visionaries that I decided to summon all my strength again and look forward to what we could accomplish in this world.

In order to fulfill my goals, I often have to work through my thoughts and plans alone. In general, I feel alone with my international vision. Sitting on the hill, I realized that I wasn't alone. I knew there weren't enough of us in the world that cared enough, but from that moment on, I never felt alone again.

Our group was told that Canada had just signed an agreement, along with Australia, New Zealand, USA, Norway and Denmark, to empty the Bhutanese refugee camps in Nepal. None of us at the time had any idea of what had happened in that region.

A young Swedish filmmaker, Anita Gustafson, spent many years in Nepal and came across some refugee camps. She made a documentary about them called "Killing Time" which won first prize at the Montreal Film Festival. She put pressure on the United Nations to do something about the situation. Some refugees had already been in those camps for twenty years. The UNHCR convinced certain countries to accept the refugees and close the camps.

Bhutan is a country which lies at the eastern end of the Himalayas. It borders China, Nepal and India. It was an absolute monarchy and is now a constitutional monarchy, headed by the king. The former king died approximately 25 years ago and his son took the throne. The new king had studied in England and came to realize that many monarchies were becoming democracies. In a democracy the majority wins. He told himself that if he wished to remain King of his country, he needed to take certain measures, one of which was to ensure that his people were homogenous.

During the reign of his great-grandfather, Nepalese had been invited to the country to cultivate uninhabited land in the south of Bhutan. He wanted his country to be self-sustaining in agricultural terms. The Nepalese came and cleared the lands and grew crops to feed the country. They were there for three generations and many of their children were Bhutanese, having being born in the country. The majority had never been to Nepal.

The newly appointed king wanted a homogenous country where all were Buddhists and all spoke Bhutanese. Most of the Nepalese were of Hindu faith and spoke Nepali.

At that time, the population of Bhutan was about 800,000 of which 116,000 were of Nepalese origin. The king imposed radical changes on the non-Buddhist minority but as they refused to accept these amendments, a territorial separation developed between the north and south of the country with the King and the local Bhutanese being the majority and located in the northern part. The king issued the

Nepalese with a deadline to change their religion, attire and mother tongue or else they would be expelled from the country. The situation deteriorated rapidly and many were imprisoned, tortured and killed; others were forced to flee the country. Nepal did not want to accept them in their country because they had already received many refugees from Tibet and they also didn't want a further imbalance of ethnicity.

The displaced turned to India but India also refused them. They had no alternative but to go to refugee camps in Nepal, close to the Nepal-Indian border. Many of these people stayed there for around twenty years.

During my time in Strasbourg, I thought it was a good idea to change the origin countries of the refugees that we were accepting to Bhutan. I spoke with the authorities in Canada and Quebec, and this was accepted. We were able to start helping the displaced Bhutanese.

I saw details of the documentary 'Killing Time' in the newspaper and called Anita and asked her to come to Saint Jerome to help us prepare for the Bhutanese refugees from Nepal.

The government told us that it would take three years to process them. I went to speak to the authorities and said, "Come on, I cannot accept leaving these people in those camps any longer. They have been stuck in those camps for twenty years".
They kept telling me that the paperwork had been signed and that they were waiting. I asked "Waiting for what?"

I kept on applying pressure and we finally received the first refugees a lot earlier than expected, in 2008.

When the first plane arrived, there were six families on board. I could see how very, very tired they were from the long trip. When I saw a lady called Bishnu, accompanied by her two daughters, I felt as if I had known her for a very long time. She was like a sister from a past life. Rupa was another young girl who was very sweet and sole carer of her younger brother and sister. I ensured that they were teamed with an experienced integration-foster family. I asked one of the fathers called Nandu, "What do you want to do in Canada?" He replied, "To become a citizen".

Their only goal was to have a passport and belong to a country.

I saw over time that the difficult part for many of the Bhutanese was adjusting to having freedom, such as freedom of thought and the freedom to marry by choice. They always spoke as 'Us' and never used the term "I" as if it didn't exist. Some still had some archaic thought and behavior patterns even after the integration process. In only one case, parents wanted to kill their daughter because she wanted to marry someone that wasn't chosen for her. Sometimes we need to spend added time with certain new arrivals, stressing that we have different codes of behavior here.

When I reflect on what the King of Bhutan did to all those people, I can only describe it as mass crime against humanity. He has never been punished for this crime. The king has a slogan that the internal revenue of his country is based on happiness. Bhutan has been referred to as "the happiest country in Asia and the 8th happiest country on earth" and yet nobody dares mention the atrocities that were committed against the ethnic Nepali minority.

The Nepalese are peaceful people and when they speak about their past, even after so many years in the camps, they don't seek revenge and many don't even appear to be angry at the king because it is not in their culture or blood to act in that way. The international community was not aware of what took place in the region for so many years.

In 2009 I went to Poland for the International Day of Peace. I had made arrangements to attend a one week conference with the Sant' Egidio Community from Rome. I witnessed first-hand how the bringing together of many religious groups could lead to peace and harmony. All were able to speak freely and easily amongst themselves and I wanted to bring that concept back with me to Saint Jerome and develop our relations with other religious communities. Since being back, I have been working on different activities to promote peace and accord in our community.

Over the years I have put a lot of work into developing the extensive gardens at the back of my house. It is a huge area. In 2013, as part of Amnesty International Day, I went to the annual ceremony where a tree was planted in the 'Place of Peace' in Saint Jerome. The tree was named "Our Sisters in Spirit." It was in honor of the 600 First Nation women who have disappeared over the years. To date, very little has been done to try and establish what happened to all these missing women.

After the ceremony, we all went for lunch which was attended by the president of Amnesty International, as well as one of the clan mothers called Madeline. One of the head Native American chiefs wanted to show me his garden in the park where there were 100 garden beds created for the community. It was beautiful. I told him that I would also like to show him the garden in our park. They all came over and he said "Hey, that's a Native American garden". Madeline and I have been great friends since that day and we have now decided that we are sisters. She has been extremely influential over recent years and has educated me about the Native American culture and how we can better relate to our First Nation people.

I learnt that there was a law in Canada that clustered the Native Americans in 'reserves' and they were forced to remain within the reserve boundaries. Some of these designated areas were big enough to enable hunting however other areas were not which impacted on what food was available. The reserves have remained in place as First Nation territories.

Many big companies that require wood or want to conduct mining activities 'steal' some of the territory from Native Americans.

Some men have also been known to kidnap Native American women, referred to as 'Squaws' and then rape and kill them. Nobody searches for the missing women to try and work out who is responsible for these appalling crimes. The Canadian police appear to be reluctant to investigate these cases.

There are military bases scattered throughout Canada and a cousin of mine was employed at one of those bases. He overheard some men talking about going out to get some 'Squaw'. They would set out to find a native woman and then group rape her. This is allowed to continue because no-one is ever arrested. It is disgusting to know that these crimes are still happening in today's society.

There is a Native American prophecy called the Eighth Fire. It developed from the tenets of the Seven Fires prophecy which dates back to before the arrival of the Europeans in Canada. It is written on Wampum, small beads utilized by the indigenous people of North America. They were used to record treaties and historical events. On each shell bead, in small symbols similar to hieroglyphics, the Wampum Prophecy is recorded.

It tells the story of the Seven Fires Prophecy. The Wampum Prophecy is separated into seven periods of time and each is referred to as a 'fire'. One of the 'fires' states that the white man would, in the future, take native children from their families and put them in homes such as orphanages to stop them from being who they were born to be. There were orphanages set up to educate children in Catholic practices and not in their Native American ways. The prophecy also stated that the white man would come on vessels and bring knowledge that would help the Native Americans evolve but it would be very dangerous if they came armed.

The Eighth Fire recommends that if all people come together and reject materialism and instead choose a path of spirituality, respect and wisdom we can avoid further environmental and social catastrophes, and this will lead to a period of spiritual illumination.

What I find interesting about the Seven Fires prophecy is that Native Americans accurately forecast what was going to happen. Historical research shows us that they have been here for at least 35,000 years, during which time they haven't polluted the land or damaged the environment. White people have been here for 500 years and have managed to pollute water and land.

I like the idea of going back to their principles. As a member of the Clan of the Turtle, I have always persevered with all projects, even those that take more than ten years to implement. I take on multiple projects at the same time and I have the energy to see each project through to the end, no matter if it takes two years or twenty years. That is what it feels like to be a turtle. I have had a fascination for turtles throughout out my life. I have a large collection of turtle sculptures and statues in my home.

In 2013 the Government of Quebec started an enquiry to formulate the fundamentals that we would need to have in place to integrate new arrivals into Quebec.

I decided to submit a proposal titled "The Champlain Charter", named after the Father of New France Samuel Champlain, who was a great explorer, cartographer and the founder of Quebec City and New France in 1608. His dream was to create a new society where people from indigenous backgrounds and all other nationalities would live together and be considered equals. His philosophy was considered to be a very new way of thinking at the time. He was convinced that this could occur when his fellow crew members went off and married Native American women. The first Chaloux married a Native American woman so I deem the connection stemmed back to Champlain's time. I believe I inherited my way of thinking from my ancestors.

I stated that if the government wished to officially document values for the people of Quebec, they must include the Native American values. I had approached a mother of one of the Native American clans and a Haitian immigrant who had been in Quebec for forty years and they both stated in my proposal that Quebec was made of people from different arrival points and that is who we are.

It was a short report because I knew that a more condensed version would be read in its entirety. I talked mainly about our community relations. I was able to present my report in parliament. One of the officials told me that I had not factored in the Muslim veil. I answered that I consider it to be a simple veil, comparing it to people wearing skull caps. I explained that a full burka is not accepted in many countries because it covers women's faces and is similar to wearing a mask.

I explained that if we wished for sound integration and democracy for all, we needed to be able to see each other's faces. I continued to point out that in the previous year, some young people had put on masks and went around destroying property in the community in a very violent manner. No one knew who they were as they were wearing masks.

I explained that we needed public security to have psychological security and no-one should be permitted to terrorize others in the streets with impunity because of masks. The same applies to zombie harassment.

I described my experience at Strasbourg in France, how we were shown a presentation from the Major General of the Canadian Army who was in Rwanda at the time of the 1993 genocide. The Canadian government refused to get involved in the war and the general was most upset by their refusal. He took many photos of what he witnessed at the time and later held an exhibition. It was horrifying to see the mutilations, women with cut breasts and scenes of unimaginable brutality. Seeing that horrific display, we all felt powerless because nobody knew how to fight against people responsible for such carnage.

I went on to explain that after the exhibition, I was in Paris and there were hundreds of people dressed as zombies scaring the public in the streets. They succeeded and there were children screaming and being extremely traumatized by the mutilated faces they saw in their local area. I felt as if I had a whole tribe of mutilated people in front of me and I couldn't understand how they could behave in this way. It seemed as if they were mocking people being massacred in some countries and I found that to be an attack on human dignity.

I am fifty-eight years old now, a mother of two children and a grandmother of two children whom I adore very much and with whom I love spending time. I am heavily involved and deeply committed to my work at the Coffret. I send two employees to greet the refugees when they arrive and at times, when I can, I go with them to welcome the new arrivals.

Line at the Coffret

When we started receiving immigrants at the end of the 1990's we had a total population of 55,000 people in Saint Jerome and in 2014, we were more than 100,000 strong. We have room to grow and develop other areas in our region if necessary. Our immigrants all manage to find jobs in different industries; some leave the area for other places, and vice versa. The whole process of integration has not been highlighted in the media because we do it peacefully, with minimal fuss and we believe that this is the reason for our integration success.

Canada accepts approximately 5,000 refugees annually of which Quebec accepts around 1800. In 2013, there were around 20 million refugees around the world waiting for placement. In 2015, there were around 60 million waiting for placement. There was an explosion of refugees over the Christmas period in December, 2013 from the wars in the Middle East. Due to the sudden intense increase in numbers, the UNHCR needs about six billion dollars urgently, just to feed all the refuges and they do not have that amount of money at their disposal. We have recently seen the situation reach a critical stage with Syria. This is the first time in Europe and the Middle East that adults and children have died from hunger in refugee camps.

Years ago, many people did not have access to weapons but now, as a result of weapon trafficking and even weapon salesmen, rebels have access to any ammunition that they want. The situation is out of control and there are groups trading weapons for commodities such as gold or petrol.

It is a terrible and totally unacceptable situation and we need to work together to protect the innocent victims. The hardest part is finding a peaceful solution. Until that happens, we have no choice as a society but to try and help the people in these countries in the best way possible whilst trying to maintain and perhaps improve the living conditions of the people who are already in our country.

Along with the COFFRET, I am currently involved in twenty-four organizations:

1 - Table of partnerships in immigration MRC RDN
2 - Advising Committee on Health
3 - Advising Committee on Education
4 - Advising Committee on Employment
5 - Regionalization committee of immigration in the Laurentians
6 - SIPPE, Integrated services of after-birth and childhood
7 - Table of concerting of refugees and immigrants
8 - Network of organizations in regionalization of immigration in Quebec
9 - Mixed Committee MIDI TCRI
10 - Community Table MRC RDN
11 - Coalition of actions in food security MRC RDN
12 - Table of homelessness of the Laurentians
13 - Lodging Committee MRC RDN
14 - Regional council of social development of the Laurentians
15 - Table of partners in immigration of Employment-Quebec
16 - Regional table on mental health
17 - Regional director committee in homelessness
18 - Local Actions Committee (CAL)
19 - Lodging "Fleur de Macadam"
20 - Cité Les 3 R
21 - Communitarian Foundation of the Laurentians
22 - Actions coalition in food security
23 - Community development corporation RDN

Line in her office at the Coffret

My mother is now 86 years of age, and apart from her, I am the only community worker in my family. My siblings all work for electrical companies including both of my sons.

We have family gatherings once a month and it is wonderful when the family comes together. I have a huge table that can be extended for large dinner parties. We discuss everything from politics to news, to everyday life and even though we don't always share the same opinions, it is nice to be able to discuss our differing views.

My ultimate goal in life, which I have had since going to Vancouver in 1986, is to live in a world of peace and harmony. I had a dream at the time in which lots of staircases were interlaced and spreading out in all directions. I was with my children walking on a staircase and could see people from all over the world around us. Some were wearing their traditional cultural costumes. They saluted us. I could see that they needed me and I knew I wanted to help them. I understood from that dream that people from every country need help of some kind and it is possible to create a global space where everyone lives in peace.

I had another dream, where I was walking through a crowded shopping center called Galeries des Laurentides. A huge lightning bolt struck, followed by deafening thunder and then the lights went out temporarily. As the lights came back on, everyone in the crowd recognized each other but we had changed. All of us were in complete awareness, having eliminated any preconceptions from the past and we remained in complete harmony from that point onwards.

I have had a great life and I know I will continue along my path and leave my legacy behind in this world. I look forward to creating the Eighth Fire throughout global communities so that youth everywhere can share their space with others, including the homeless and create a place of assembly where there is no judgment and everyone lives in solidarity. Professional educators and healers could use these gatherings to meet people and help them. Together, as compassionate individuals, we can achieve greatness and peacefully live together in a better world.

Chapter XVI

Moving Forward – Angelique Papadelias

As a result of these amazing stories, many wonderful things have happened to me. I have seen hope in people's eyes. I have seen individuals and groups opening their hearts to help others. I have cherished this exceptional opportunity to tell the stories of these amazing people and to be the catalyst for change in some people's lives.

If you enjoyed reading these stories, please share them with your network, reach out to media personnel or to any bloggers that you know and help us get this book out there to the world audience. We need your support to make this project a great success!

A decent percentage of the royalties from this book will go directly to help refugees in the local community and also towards funding a project that I am working on that requires research, dedicated individuals and a proactive team that work towards enabling orphans to have a better future. This book is about understanding, caring and giving back to others who share this world with us: a world that has been a sacred zone for me to live in. I hope that in time we can make it a sacred zone for all refugee families globally.

You are welcome to like the book on facebook and the author at:
www.angeliquepapadelias.com
www.littlescreenbigscreen.com
www.faithinourfreedom.com